Savage Awakening

Savage Awakening

INITIATORY PATHS OF THE DRAGON MOTHER

SADEE WHIP

First Edition **ISBN**-979-8-9883580-0-8

E book   **ISBN**-979-8-9883580-1-5

Audiobook   **ISBN**-979-8-9883580-2-2

DRAGON MOTHER MEDIA

Olympia, Washington

THEDRAGONMOTHER.COM

I thank the
many forms
of the
Dragon Mother the
mighty
individual
Beings
fragments
of Her one Being I
kneel in
awe that
She
reveals aspects for
each and every
need we might have I
writhe at Her
incomprehensible
penetration
I bow in devotion and
tremble in
fear I
shake with Her
breath on my
neck my
reverence
as vast as the sky
my astonished spirit
Hers

The Body of This Book

Foundation, Orientation, and a Dragon

The Field of Denial and a Map of Reality

The Three Fold Nature of Initiation

The Four Paths

Three phases of the Initiatory Path

The Unseen Realm

Tidbits and Tools

INTRODUCTION

There is a way that people are called, are pulled, are gnawed at, by an invisible force. For some of us it is there our whole lives. For others, it's like a distant, haunting song. And for others still, it is a brutal awakening to the realization that what we thought was reality is not, that we can never return, and we have nowhere else to go.

Searches in Buddhism or crystal healing or Wicca or Tantra or alternative anything never quite cut it. It's like you've fallen through a crack no one can quite explain, into a territory with no map. It can be lonely, exhilarating, confusing, or traumatizing - sometimes all at once.

You will search desperately for answers as to what is happening to you and what it means. It is likely you will question your sanity and feel desperate to find someone who will not only think you are not crazy, but who will actually be able to help you understand what is happening to you.

In this way, you will likely have spent countless hours and many more dollars going from person to person seeking "healing" or understanding, and not really getting it, while likely internalizing your experience to the point where you question yourself in an unsettling way.

Or maybe you have found your niche, discovered what is

going on and what you are, yet you struggle to navigate the world - to pay bills, make a living, and belong somewhere – sometimes just barely *functioning* in this society that is so out of sync with Truth.

In my private practice of more than 30 years, I have encountered enough people going through the exact experiences that I describe in this book to understand that there is a deeper phenomenon happening than what, on the surface, looks like "personal growth".

There is a pattern in our struggles. A pattern of a certain kind of awareness accompanied by a feeling of being compelled or taken up by a force one cannot ignore. A feeling of a deeper call of Life that pulls us from the comfortable attempts to belong in society, onto a path that is largely unacknowledged. A path where we may question our sanity, feel scared about what, exactly, is pulling us, and feel threatened we may "lose everything". It is clear that we are becoming something we had not anticipated.

The journey is different for each of us, but the terrain is the same. And that's one of the things I am going to map in this book for you - the terrain.

I am going to show you what is happening so you can understand, with the deep belief and lifetime of experience that I have, that understanding will save you a lot of suffering and struggle.

I am also going to talk about what is required of us at each stage of the map, a kind of "how it works" as a human becoming something more than just human.

What is revealed here will not apply to every person who feels pulled. Some of you do not have the Wyrd, or the fate, to walk this path. Rejoice - for you will be spared a great deal of hardship. This does not mean what is here will not be useful at all - though how useful only you can say.

For those of you who do have the Wyrd that compels you to be on this path, rejoice! For there is no greater blessing, no greater adventure, no more profound way of being that I can think of if your feet are meant for this path.

I believe that there is something happening that has either increased in intensity or simply come out of the shadows of history: I believe that the deeper forces of Life, the very alive Intelligence that is the fabric of reality itself, is enlisting those of us who are good candidates for something quite necessary. I believe this Intelligence has many names and I believe it is both very personal and deeply impersonal in the paradoxical way of truly ancient Beings.

You do not need to believe in these Beings as I do, at least, not yet. Indeed, many Westerners have been conditioned to feel unintelligent if they claim too real a belief in anything other than science or "The Universe" as a very generic, and safe, way of speaking about the obvious Intelligence that permeates the world around us.

For those who are truly called to this path, you will eventually be required to have a more personal relationship with this Intelligence and will need to move beyond the conditioned mind into a respectful, reciprocal relationship with the Unseen Beings of this world. You will need this in order to not only move forward, but to survive what this path is and where it leads. In this way, you become what you truly are.

This path undoes us. Each passage of our undoing makes way for ever increasing amounts of something else to come through. That something else is what we seek, and what seeks us. We are becoming truly liminal, truly alive, truly free, truly powerful, and truly, something else.

The Unseen Intelligence of Life begins, more and more, to see and act and think through us. In this way, we become doorways for these energies to come into the world and have impact - needed, necessary, essential impact. And as this Intelligence comes through us, we learn more about the Being at the heart of it All. I call this Being The Dragon Mother.

This will make more sense as we go, but if you feel resonance with this, it is not a coincidence that you have found this book.

Many pathways exist for the kind of transformation and connection I speak of. But one thing is certain, you must shift from the conditioning of independence into the reality of interdependence, you must become deeply, profoundly relational. Indeed, becoming relational *is* walking the path, until you reach the edge of the map in this book, then make your own wild way.

This is not "personal growth". This is coming to wholeness in a way that tears the perceptual limitation between you and the deeper forces of this world. It is skin-shedding, shape shifting, howling, storm riding. And what you must do, the only thing you must do, is keep going, even when you can't.

Walking this path is not about your personal goals, desires, wounds, or preferences. Walking this path is not about *you* at all. This means there will be much fear, teeth gnashing, confusion, and, yes, profound joy. For as you become something else, a new meaning will arise, a meaning beyond personal fulfillment. You will discover the immense radiant state of belonging in the unfathomably vast and complex web of existence. You will discover what lies beyond the small bubble of human and the relief that can only be found in the paradox of full accountability and utter surrender.

But before that, there is work to do, fields to traverse, wonders to discover, and demons to meet.

Part One:

Foundation, Orientation, and a Dragon

One

SAVAGE AWAKENING

"Can you make me a potion?" the message says. I can feel her through the screen - powerful, swirling, disoriented. She feels on the verge of exploding or imploding, I cannot tell. So I am careful. I breathe and type "Of course. What are you thinking?"

We have never spoken before this.

She announces she's gone to my website and read everything and wants to know who I am and what I do. I can tell she needs help. *Strange* help.

After we go back and forth for a bit, I suggest we have a brief phone call to connect to get a feel for each other and see what happens. She agrees.

The next day we are talking. She is intense, tentative, like a pacing animal looking at me from the corners of her eyes.

She starts off telling me how tentative she is because she has shared her story with so many people and no one has been able to help her make sense of it. She's afraid that will happen with me and she can't bear it. She needs help. I can feel she is drowning in the tidal swirl of her own becoming.

So we talk.

Her story is familiar, yet utterly unique to her:

She has been on a path. She has "abilities". She is deeply connected to something she calls "The Life Force". Some strange things have been happening and she got sucked into a reality that is utterly out of time and place with this one. She doesn't know what is happening but she knows it's mythic. She knows I might think she's crazy. She knows whatever is happening it's important but she can't tell why yet because she isn't clear what is even going on.

"Can you help me? Do you understand? Am I crazy? Is this all just crazy?"

It is a plea I have heard many, many times.

A plea that is utterly in line with a pattern I have been seeing for decades. A pattern that reveals a phenomenon that I believe is quite ancient but one we either no longer believe is possible or has been ground into oblivion by powers that would have it concealed. A phenomenon we often only hear about in folklore. A phenomenon that modern society would have us believe is not real.

And yet, I have seen it play out over and over in the people I work with. And in people I have had the great fortune to connect with over these many years of my own wandering. It is a phenomenon that seems to be increasing in occurrence. I call it "Savage Awakening".

Savage   Awakening   is   not   "enlightenment"   or

"transcendence". Savage Awakening is what happens to those of us that *belong* to the Great Mother, even as we might know Her by different names and guises. Savage Awakening is what happens to those of us that came forth into this world from the Mystery, to be Emissaries of that Wisdom - to be the hands and heartbeats of Her.

Savage Awakening is what you go through as you come into the realization of what you are and the conflict this creates with the world around you - the tension of not belonging in the world as created by humans coupled with the immensity of the process of moving towards What is calling you.

Savage Awakening is the process of leaving what you once were and becoming something entirely different. You become more. You become a multiplicity. You become a part of the Primal Reality itself and dwell amongst the beings of Primal Truth in a state of extraordinary connection in an utterly respectful, reciprocal relationship. And in this way you may gain access to extraordinary things.

In a nutshell, it's a trip.

It can make you feel insane, sick, like you are going to die. It can make you feel the holiness of Life, of yourself. It can make you feel power and beauty beyond all comprehension.

It feels urgent, and more important than anything, that whatever is happening to you be allowed to happen. Like your life depends on it.

But how?

How can we, as modern people, live the secret truth of ourselves as Emissaries of these Deep Powers in a world that values speed and money and man-made shiny things? How can we pay our bills, have conversations, participate in the falseness?

Short answer?

We don't.

I mean, we do and we don't. You can certainly survive in a modern way - pay your bills, buy groceries, drive your car. But we cannot *live* in that world as that world would have us live in it.

This is where so much of the initial tension of beginning to wake-up comes from - of admitting to yourself what you really are.

This is the tension of Initiation.

Two

THE INVISIBLE PATH

Central to the process of Savage Awakening is the experience of Initiation. I want to talk about this a bit so we can lay a foundation of context for what is to come, as it is very likely you are already well into this experience.

Initiation is, by definition, the rites, ceremonies, ordeals, or instructions with which one is made a member of a sect or society or is invested with a particular function or status. You will come to see that the initiations of the Dragon Mother largely serve a particular function.

I call initiation the Invisible Path. Invisible because we often cannot see it, have no idea where it will lead, and others often deny or invalidate it. It is a path because it absolutely does lead somewhere. Where it leads depends on you, how deep you are called to the Dragon Mother, and how far you are able to go.

Savage Awakening is the initiation. In modern society, it feels like an act of self-initiation - after all, we are the ones experiencing strange things, usually by ourselves, because of the things we feel drawn to, the thoughts we have, the dreams we have, the ways our eyes and hearts begin to see. It feels very much like an internal process.

This feeling, as if we are in a kind of self-initiation, is a product of our conditioning. It is the result of the disconnection that is foundational to modern human society, what I call The Field of Denial.

The truth is, the initiation we go through is made possible by natural and strange forces that we are already in relationship with, which slowly, or quite suddenly in some cases, make themselves known to us.

Initiation is, in most cases, fairly awful. You might have said things like "I'm getting my ass kicked", "I cannot get a break", "I don't know how much more I can take". It might also show up as a major life event that utterly strips you bare - a major loss, a huge shift or roadblock on your path, or an unexpected and unwelcome mental burden, like depression.

Initiation *always* shifts us away from our normal lives and initiation *always* makes our ability to function in the "normal" world challenging.

This is absolutely essential to the process of awakening. Not because suffering is some noble thing or trauma is essential to being spiritual. But because we as a human society have gotten so far away from what is real and essential that we dwell in a state of disconnection as normal, celebrated, and valued.

We have turned away from the interconnected web of life and gone off and made our own little bubble of a kind of insane asylum we call "society" that functions on a premise, a necessity, of disconnection.

We have made disconnection a kind of status symbol. How many people do you have power over? How much do you control? How much more do you have? How much better looking are you? How much forest can you burn? How many animals can you enslave? How many homeless or hurt beings can you walk right by and not notice? How many trees can you cut down and not hear scream?

In fact, we are so disconnected we do not even notice these questions. We simply live with the invisible permeation of disconnection and play by the implied rules it carries.

The proof of this disconnection-made-normal lies very simply in the fact that people who "care too much" are labeled "sensitive" or "dramatic" or "weak" or "hippie", or many other terms meant to be derogatory, for the fact that they are exhibiting a care and feeling of responsibility toward other beings beyond the very narrow limits of hyper-normalized selfishness that pervades modern society.

And so we must be pulled from this insanity. This is part of the purpose Initiation serves.

Please understand that it is not us pulling ourselves from the Field of Denial. It *is*, however, us cooperating with the pull.

Here is what I mean:

At some point in the initiatory process, one *sees through* the mirage of the Field of Denial (we discuss Field of

Denial in Part 2). This *seeing through* may be a felt sensation, a discomfort, a pain, a sense that something isn't right, that things don't make sense, that the way people behave is bizarre and they act like it's not-bizarre. We may also simply bear witness to so much atrocity or coldness or disconnection that we know, somewhere deep in the center of who we are, that this is wrong.

Some of us may still carry the truth we came into this world with, the truth all children carry, that life is connected and we are all in deep relationship together. Those of us that never lost connection to this truth may find we have had to fight in various ways, and to various degrees, to retain this truth and not lose it. Others of us perhaps have forgotten this truth or buried it and our initiation involves remembering and dealing with the reverberations and implications of remembering.

At some point on this path, we are able to *see*. We see through the normalizing of the Field of Denial that we have been conditioned into.

At the moment of this conscious witnessing of the insanity of this world, we send out a pulse, a signal, from our being.

This signal reaches the web of life and it reaches the beings that exist in spite of the Field of Denial and it activates, in a way that is like a cry for help or a kind of permission, Their help. (The truth is, They are always there, it is simply that we become open to Them because we get to a place where Their aid is required and we are desperate enough to allow ourselves to need Their help, which is mostly taboo in the modern world.)

No matter how hard the Initiation experience is you are going through, please understand that behind it is an answer to your call for help and many beings of the Deeper Reality of life are responding to your call to try to help you escape the Field of Denial and, in this way, move toward coming into wholeness.

Your call for help potently activates the Deeper Forces of life to connect with you because you get cracked open via the process of initiation to allow for the necessity of Them. Without this cracking open, without the desperation it brings, few among us would be able to allow in the help we need. Our need must be desperate.

Why, then, is Initiation often so very painful? So difficult? And, for some of us, genuinely life-threatening?

First and foremost let me say that there are powers far wiser than you or I at play here - beings far more ancient. Which means we are not always going to understand. This truth can be quite uncomfortable, to say the least. Especially in the beginning of your Initiation experience.

To understand why initiation is so painful, we need to understand what purpose it serves.

Modern humans have gotten so far away from Primal Reality, i.e. *What Is,* that we have utterly turned our backs on the interwoven nature of existence that is the very fabric of reality itself.

At some point, I suspect as far back as the dawn of civilization, for reasons unknown, humans turned away from the relational nature of life, the sacredness of all things, and the Intelligence that is existence itself.

As Robin Artisson states in his book The Secret History, *"This turning away - this great disease of the spirit that reflects into our every action, thought, feeling, and activity - is the true cause of all the miseries and the deep sense of existential alienation we have suffered individually and collectively ever since. This might be considered one of the mystery-revelations that civilizations cannot tolerate at too public a level within their midst."*

He refers to this as a "great disease of spirit" and I couldn't agree more.

Now we begin to see why Initiation is so painful - because we are being ripped out of the Field of Denial, stripped of the many layers of conditioning that are embedded in our flesh and mind, that permeate our very essence with a disease most humans do not realize they have. And we do this in a society that is heavily invested in our continued participation in its sickness. It is a very difficult predicament.

Initiation, then, partially serves the process of leaving the Field of Denial and being transformed into a being that can understand, and participate in, the deeper mysteries of life. Initiation is the process that sets us firmly on the path of being capable of relationship within the context of the Primal Reality - a kind of return, as much as a modern human is capable, to our deepest, most ancient, most holy roots.

This transformation into something new is composed of at least one death. For most of us, we die again and again and again to our old way of being. We are stripped of the coping mechanisms that allow us to be adapted to the Field of Denial and are left with no available resources within that reality.

This place of "no available resources within that reality" may feel like a kind of hell. Indeed, it is scary, disorienting, and lonely. But it is also exactly where we need to be in order to turn toward other resources - to even have it occur to us to seek something different than that found in the Field of Denial.

We effectively need to feel, and be, kicked out of modern society in such a way that we can undergo the necessary process of transformation that initiation brings.

The lonely terror of this experience is not one that has to be so very awful. And this is precisely why I am writing this book for you. It will serve as your handbook as you navigate these dark, mysterious, sometimes treacherous, often incredibly beautiful waters of transformation.

For now, take comfort in the fact that your Initiation experience is happening *because* other beings are seeking to connect with you as much as you are seeking to connect with what lies beyond the Field of Denial. You are, in fact, not alone.

And herein lies a key to your journey: Relationship. More precisely, learning to be in right-relationship with the beings that inhabit the broader, more potent reality of *What Is.*

As long as we are together through these pages, I will be helping you as much as I am able in this space with what you may encounter and how to skillfully walk this Invisible Path. May it ease your discomfort and perhaps bring a measure of peace as you are torn apart.

Three

YOU ARE BORN TO THIS PATH

In the last chapter Initiation was defined as: the rites, ceremonies, ordeals, or instructions with which one is made a member of a sect or society or is invested with a particular function or status.

Many kinds of initiation can be pursued, or given, or chosen. The initiation of the Dragon Mother is not this kind of initiation.

My experience, both personally for myself as well as with the many people I have encountered on this path, is that those of us called by the Dragon Mother are born to Her.

The realization of this can be something that comes later in life. But for many of us, we have known, without frameworks perhaps, that we belong to, that we serve, something else in this life - that our lives are not our own in the way they are for other people. We have a sense of duty or need or a kind of compulsion that causes us to engage the world in ways that seem unusual to others or that we recognize are not shared by others.

The way this feels inside oneself, and how we can understand it as being different from moral or religious indoctrination and obligation is this:

It is almost like having a voice or another mind inside of yourself that reveals things, almost like narrating your experiences. A mind that causes you to notice things others don't. A view of the world that stimulates an urge in oneself to *do something* about the things that are revealed by this other Intelligence. A mind that is so warm, so...loving almost, that it feels indistinguishable from our closest family. Closer even.

For most of us, we don't even notice it is there until we reach an age where we can distinguish the lived reality of others enough to understand that this Intelligence is not alive in them.

Alive. Aliveness. That is a key feature of being born to this path - there is an irrepressible aliveness in those of us who belong to it. It is as if some disproportionately large allotment of life force was siphoned into us and we came into the world with the need to dispense it. This isn't merely a dispersal of this energy, but an imperative for that life force to go to the places where it is needed.

Until we are further on this path, we may have not even had a conscious awareness of this fact about ourselves.

This is beyond the need to "help". It is a feeling that if we do not allow this force to go where it is needed that our life itself will have less meaning - that we cannot feel satisfied or fulfilled or happy if this state of being a kind of conduit, or this state of being relational with this Intelligence, is not being lived.

It's not that the particular flavor of this life force is what we must do for a living, but it often becomes the only way we can actually survive without being miserable or feeling empty. It is also often the only way we can actually belong in society - by figuring out how to vocationally be a conduit in some way. This is, in fact, a key to our success in surviving this Initiation in a modern world.

I have often described this as "being a vessel for how Life wants to be in the world through you".

Something that will likely significantly help you on this path is to think of yourself as a vessel or a conduit for the Deeper Intelligence. It is a very helpful first step in becoming instantly more relational. Being relational, as we will see, is essential, absolutely essential, for walking, and surviving, this path.

As you conceive of yourself as a vessel-conduit, you can begin to notice the flavor and texture of how Deeper Intelligence feels different from how you feel to yourself. When does it show up? Where do you feel it in your body? How is this different than when you have your own thoughts and urges about things?

The more you practice this noticing, the more you are in a position to come into more personal relationship with this Intelligence. The more personal relationship you can come into, the less confusion there will be between your conditioning, your fear, the noise and condemnation of Christian culture (or whatever religion dominates your upbringing), and the non-allowance of this kind of relationship and the transformation and power that often comes with it.

I have yet to meet someone who was not born to this path be able to follow it. I am not Queen of the Universe or the All Knowing Whip, but I have consciously been on this path, studied this path, been devoted to this path, since I pledged myself to it at the tender age of seven. As of this writing, that is 47 years of walking this path. I've encountered tens of thousands of people in these many decades and I have yet to encounter someone not chosen by Her who showed the signs, patterns, and particular *je ne sais quoi* of those born to this path.

It is not lost on me that we all want to feel special at some point in our life. And I get that the idea of "being chosen" or having a patron deity or that any version of these is something many of us covet. So let me shed some light on what it is like to be born to this path.

First and foremost, your life is not your own. You are in a kind of sacred obligation to a Being that is far more ancient and incomprehensible than you can imagine. This obligation gets increasingly revealed as you go down this path and you will wrestle with it on more levels than you can conceive.

The Being you are obligated to may never, ever show its face to you. You will live with uncertainty, confusion, outsider-ness, and moments of intensity that would blow the circuits of most humans. You will be tried, over and over and over. You will finally get the hang of the place you are in, the rules and the tempo, then get two seconds of rest and orientation and solace only to wake up the next day to the next phase of your journey and have to start all over with not knowing who or what you are or what the f**k you are supposed to be doing with yourself. There is no target to hit and, when you think there is, you will be the butt of the joke when, with ever-growing humility, you have to examine where you are still holding on to the idea of "knowing" anything and where you still need to work on responding to the ever-unfolding moment that is this life.

You will continually be led by breadcrumbs that you will follow with varying degrees of hope and that you will always hunger for. Those breadcrumbs will almost never lead you to the place you want or hope for but will always contain some portion of what you need in a kind of supralogical sequence you will never, ever, be able to map.

Do not wish for this path. Do not try to force yourself to walk it out of some feeling of specialness. A key characteristic of this path is that what you are will be destroyed in more ways than you knew were possible and, if you are fortunate, will be replaced by things you never knew existed that will bring you into the relational fold of belonging that is at once the warmest, most beautifully solid thing you will ever experience and the most intangible coldness possible.

This path will split you apart, tear you asunder, and destroy you. That is the entire purpose. This is not Love or Enlightenment or Heaven. This is intimacy with Primal Reality. This is pursuing, out of torturous need, the Dragon Mother - the great being known in Her most ancient form as the Great Serpent, or as the Mother of the Great Serpent. What that is for you, how that looks and feels and plays out, is between you and Her. All I can do is alert you to what I have mapped and what I have discovered and what I have created to navigate the fact of it.

The specialness you uncover on this path will have more to do with the mind-blowing fact of Creation and the terrifying beauty of experiencing it than anything to do with you. For when you do realize how incredibly special and unique and wondrous you are, it simply won't matter anymore, because the person to whom that was relevant will no longer exist in any kind of substantial way.

This journey is a path of wholeness. Not of *you* becoming whole - that is a small wholeness. It is the wholeness of the entire existence, where the Dragon Mother molds and shapes you into a vessel for Her to be in the world through you and to act in the world through you - where you exist to enact Her wishes in the world more directly - spirit made matter and matter acting on and within matter. For any human, in any time in history, this is the ultimate purpose initiation serves - wholeness of the web, where matter and spirit come into alignment with shared purpose and meaning. Where the individual ceases to be and is replaced (formed into via initiation) by the fractal reality of Her.

A final note: It is okay if you, right now, have a need or desire to be special. You can be born to this path and carry that need or desire both at the same time. Our next chapter will help you with how to do this and so much more.

Four

BE WHERE YOU REALLY ARE

Perhaps more important than anything else I can say about your path is this:

BE WHERE YOU REALLY ARE.

It is a mistake to think that we are heading for a destination of some kind. It is also a mistake to think we are the acting agents in our life, the creators, the magicians.

I know the words above may be met with resistance. Those who are deep enough on their path, or simply just tired of fighting, will recognize the truth in them.

What you will come to see is that we, in the great spiritual ecosystem of existence, are not the wisest beings. There is an Intelligence - an ancient force that has given rise to trees and oceans and stars and fish - that is beneath, within, and acting upon, all that we are.

As Frater Archer says in the concluding wisdom of his book Holy Daimon: *"Our role in this journey is not to be the protagonist, but the substance that is acted upon. We are not the alchemist, but the powder in the flask. We are not the mason, but the raw stone in the quarry. Nature is the wisest being of all....All we need to do is create the right conditions so that this process can happen right here, right now. May the art and the artist be united perfectly within us."*

We do this precisely through the practice of BE WHERE YOU REALLY ARE.

As it becomes a mantra, a way of being, it has a way of radically shifting our own becoming. This is precisely because, in order to do this very thing, we must step outside the internal critic, the conditioning, the shoulds, the judgments, the contorting, the self-flagellation, the perfectionism, the control, the blame, the shame, the accomplisher, and, yes, the morality of our times..

The dominant approach found in our society that we all seem to agree, or assume, is correct, is a process of "healing and fixing" that aims at becoming something other than what we are in that moment.

As you will learn, a core of Savage Awakening is growing big enough to hold the Paradox of Existence. So we will start here with a small paradox for you to wrestle with:

"Be where you really are" is to sit with the truth of yourself **as you are** in any particular moment - with the judgment, shame, the pain, the fragility - all *without resigning yourself to what you find and without the urge to fix it the moment it is experienced.*

The essence of this practice is to release the need to have to become something else. Again, without resigning yourself to what you really are in any moment.

But how do we do this? And why?

It is my observation that people waste an extraordinary amount of time by the socially justified, even revered, method of "working on oneself".

It goes something like this....

There is a better/ideal/right version of me that I can and should achieve. This version is made up of the opposites of the things I have an aversion to in myself. If I am unattractive, I will become beautiful. If I am angry, I will walk with Buddah-like serenity. If I am unhealthy, I will become vibrant and full of energy. If I am small and weak, I will become so mighty that no one can hurt me.

Take a minute and think about what ideal self you have created as your "goal" for what you will look like after you have worked on yourself and are finally "healed". Perhaps, after reading the last chapter, you idealize the More Self as your goal.

Please understand that for each person there is some hint of this image, this goal, being created from what we have aversions to in ourselves - from our inability to accept who and what we are and recoiling from this by creating some version of not-that. Then spending our time constantly comparing ourselves to it, judging ourselves against it, beating ourselves up for it, and throwing our resources of time and energy and money at trying to achieve it.

The huge, invisible flaw with this is that we never stop to consider that we are trying to be our best selves by utterly rejecting and condemning what we actually are in a particular moment. This creates a tension in us that keeps us on a veritable hamster wheel of seeking or working-on.

For many of us, what gets lost in all of this is the simple fact of the vulnerability, innocence, and pain that we carry. We want to be something else because we want ease or respite from the pain and vulnerability. We rarely talk about this or admit this because "being enlightened" has a lot more social collateral. At the very least, it's easier to talk about.

Being where you really are is a completely different approach. It is an approach not based on becoming what you imagine you should look like, but of sitting with yourself in a way that what you find loses its sting and the tension of judgment and shame fall away, creating space for compassion and gentleness and curiosity to arise - creating space for you to just exist as you are without your existence being somehow wrong.

Further, being where you really are makes space to suddenly exist in more of a system of relationships than in isolation. When you practice being where you really are, you begin to see how much of your moods, health, and overall well-being are affected by the systems you belong to and participate in. You no longer see that you must crack the whip on yourself to not feel certain things, but that you must become more deeply integrated with the life around you, and it with you, in order to truly be well.

This changes the game significantly. And while it may seem enlightening or relieving to read, the actual practice is often terrifying.

Being where you really are means sitting face-to-face with your fears. Looking into the weak, shameful, lame, raging, ugly, innocent, soft, hurtable bits. It means sitting with an ocean of other people's not so loving comments that they believe are truths about us - facing them, feeling into them, trying them on, and deciding what we think and feel about them before deciding to do, or not do, anything about them.

We are, all of us, running from the parts of ourselves that others did not love sufficiently, and that we, in turn, did not ourselves learn how to love. We are, all of us, turning away from things in ourselves that have simply not been tenderly allowed.

To love sufficiently does not merely mean "enough" it also means "well". Quantity and quality both. I would suggest that neither the insecure self-loathing among us, nor the greedy, overly-confident were loved sufficiently. Few of us are in the context of a healthy system in which we find belonging, not just in our immediate families, but in the society in which we happen to live.

I am not suggesting you need to love all the parts of yourself. I am suggesting you need to be willing to experience not having an aversion to things that are in you. And that you do this with an understanding that this is often not a solo journey. Very often what needs healing also needs witnessing by others and it can be painfully difficult to let others witness what we hold aversions to within ourselves.

Being where you really are is, as I said, stepping outside of conditioning. This includes moral conditioning. How can you possibly know what you really are, in any kind of a way that leads to security and orientation and rootedness, if you spend your time and energy and resources running from what you have an aversion to in yourself?

Very often in our society we cultivate a kind of armor that, when it finally grows into our skin, we feel we can say "I used to be this, but no longer!" and think that this is being where we really are.

No, being where you really are is raw. It is unarmored and very personal and intensely honest. And it must be based in the knowing that underneath all of the pain or illusions of power that there is something innocent and vulnerable in each of us. And that it is the disrespect shown to this innocence and vulnerability that has caused so very many of our issues.

Why, then, would you do anything other than show deep care and respect to yourself as you gaze upon the hurt, the conditioning, the patterns, the defenses, the trauma, the baggage, the pride, and the shame if you understand what is underneath it all? Why would you hurt yourself with judgment and condemnation and the commitment to be not-yourself? And why, oh why, would you try to become something other than what you are when you have not faced the raw truth of yourself? Have not been transformed by the honesty of non-infiltrated gazing?

Be where you really are means to stop running. It means to stop generating the illusion that you are really doing work on yourself when what you are doing is everything you can to avoid your innocence and vulnerability. Being where you really are is to look at yourself with a kind of gentle curiosity "What is really here? What am I really? What has happened to me that has made me these ways? What care do I need? What does it mean that I am _____? What do I want it to mean? What if I let go of meaning, what then?"

There can be no freedom, no true power, no real awakening, no true growth, if you cannot sit and face yourself over and over and over until all stigma, all judgment, all sting is gone.

Be where you really are is a practice, sometimes lifelong, but certainly a skill you must cultivate if you are to leave the realm of your own small universe, leave the realm of the human created, and step into the greater ecosystem of the Seen and Unseen realms.

Being where you really are underlies true freedom, and true belonging.

So how might one do this?

You can start with what I share below, and practice this until you really get the hang of it. Then come up with your own ways. Just do not come up with them too quickly or they will likely be composed of things your sneaky little protector self will use to avoid the agony of peeling off layers of pain-skin and standing naked and exposed in the cool, strong wind of your own soul.

Practice:

Start with noticing.

Notice when and how and where you get stimulated into self-judgment, condemnation, flagellation or excess pride, arrogance, anger, etc. Where do you feel this in your body? What thoughts go with the feeling?

Notice what you do with it. What self-talk do you go into? Do you convince yourself you're right/fine/better? Do you judge and then label then chastise? Do you correct yourself, clench your jaw, get angry with yourself? Do you feel a flood of shame then the rising of the defensive shield then turn to blame to get away from your detestable vulnerability or weakness? Do you feel anxious? Disoriented? Small? Alone?

Just notice. And take note. Mentally, or in a journal if that's your style, log when you go into your judgment or pride with yourself.

After you have noticed for some time and are quite good at identifying when, where, and how your buttons get activated, go and sit quietly by yourself.

Sit with it.

What you are going to do now is to take the feeling you have identified that you have an aversion to or a defensive need for and say "Okay, this is me. I have this in me. I carry a lot of _____ (i.e. pride, misery, shame, clumsiness, ugliness, grossness, condescending, evil, etc.)"

Then let yourself settle into it like a new piece of furniture. Just settle in and see what it feels like. Resist the urge to be moralistic about it. Resist the urge to decide what it means about you. Resist the urge to create a future image of yourself, either how you need to be instead or what will become of you if you don't change.

And then notice some more. Notice what the various parts of you begin to do in the face of this aspect of yourself.

What parts are speaking? What are they saying? What does your body feel like looking at this, sitting with this aspect of what you are? What fears arise?

Again, notice. Notice all the voices, all the feelings.

And then say again "This is me. Right now. This is me. So what?"

And then notice. Notice what beliefs arise with this. So you're unlovable? So you are disgusting? So you are better than everyone around you? So what?

The point is to work your way to the stories you have that live underneath the judgments and defensive constructs. Then to have those stories fall away. Not because you are "working on them" but because falling away of untruths is what happens in the presence of gentle noticing.

Learn about yourself.

In this space you will begin to see and hear and feel the pain you have been living with that has been buried under your constructed compensations and techniques. And in this way you may have compassion for yourself begin to arise. Or, at least, less of an attachment to being so harsh on yourself or perhaps so egotistical.

Once you can do this with yourself a bit, perhaps you become more honest with others. Perhaps you begin to let others see you and give yourself the opportunity to be transformed by the honesty of this space?

In our quick-fix culture let me just say, this practice is one you will likely engage for years. It will reveal depth and nuance and it will allow you to soften into acceptance of yourself and others. Do not be in a rush, for that, too, is simply the old self, the old way.

If you get nothing else from this book, may this one practice be one you take and carry with you.

When you begin to reap the benefits of Be Where You Really Are, you will begin to notice that you become naturally less judgmental and naturally more curious. This will open a creative stream in you and it will open you more to the influence of Life's Intelligence. It will help you to become what you might be in stark contrast to the you you have tried to create from your aversions. And in this way you will feel a peace and a spaciousness quite profound.

Beware of the sneaky tendency to make a goal of this. Beware of making this a competition or of the idea that there is a "right way" to do this or that there is somewhere to get to. With this practice you are developing the ability to really feel, in an embodied way, the stories and experiences you live within as well as the subtle, and sometimes profound, effect experiencing yourself without moral/judgmental/conditioned lenses will have on you.

This practice has the effect of causing the Field of Denial to lose its grip on you. And you will find yourself beginning to quite naturally migrate towards its edges and getting glimpses of other realities, other possibilities, beyond its borders.

Then you get to shift from fighting your aversions and preferences with yourself to fighting for your right to *be* as you *are*.

Do not make the mistake so many in modern society make: That your thoughts about this are what it will actually be. Thinking ain't doing. Give yourself the gift of not knowing. Give yourself the gift of curiosity. Give yourself the gift that someone might be able to help you without you controlling it or understanding it or somehow knowing more than they do. Just try it out and notice what happens, and that includes utterly sucking at it and taking months to even be able to feel where in your body you are holding patterns or emotions. There is nowhere to get to. There is only the experience and the transformation that comes from having the experience that neither you nor I can predict.

What arises from this practice is foundational to belonging and it profoundly enables the process of becoming.

Five

BECOMING

Savage Awakening is not linear. Meaning you do not progress from one stage to another following a series of steps. In truth, no personal or spiritual growth is linear.

This is important to understand, no matter where you are, because modern society has embedded within it an invisible assumption that growth is linear. Some growth is, but that kind of growth is largely physical. "Becoming" is certainly not a linear experience.

Why this is important is because you need to know what to expect, and you need to be able to understand how the frameworks that you operate in contribute greatly to, not only the fact of your becoming, but, the degree to which you suffer while you experience it.

If you expect to go from "waking up to the Field of Denial" → moving to the edge of it → to getting out → etc. → etc. →etc. you will be in for some major agony.

You are not linear. The experience of being is not linear. Your interactions with Life are not linear.

Have you ever "dealt with an issue" - like you became aware you had an issue then you worked on it, maybe went to therapy, understood and processed it, began to behave differently, *felt* different, only to find yourself in a situation where suddenly that issue is back like it never went anywhere at all? Like you didn't actually do any work on it all? Where you are just as co-dependent or just as petty or just as freaky as you were in the past in a particular moment and you cannot even believe the issue is still there?

This is an example of multidimensionality versus linearity.

And this is why it is so incredibly important to really break the habit of thinking in terms of "progress".

First Things First: Perspective

It is crucial to understand that we all have certain perspectives that inform our experience of reality. These perspectives are like lenses we look through that determine what we see, how we interpret, and what we experience.

Think of these perspectives as stories we live in and assumptions we make based upon things like our culture, our family stories, our conditioning, our fears, our beliefs - all these and more color the way we see and experience reality.

We could say that the perspective we have determines the experiences we have. It's like that thing when you decide to buy a car. You do research for the car that best fits your needs and you realize a Subaru fits the bill. Suddenly you start seeing Subarus everywhere. Are there more Subarus than before you decided to buy one? No. Your lens, your perspective, is oriented toward Subarus so you experience more of them.

Now, the society in which we live has lenses as well. For example, the notion of "independence". In the US where I live, independence has come to mean "not needing" and we view needing with such disdain that the majority of people you encounter here could not even tell you what they need beyond food/shelter/air/water/clothing. Some might say "love" but that's as far as you'll usually get. (Other needs, just to put this out there: dignity, autonomy, respect, mutual aid, inclusion, peace, structure, acknowledgement...the list goes on and these are as basic and valid as air and shelter and clothing and food)

I want you to imagine what happens when we, in this book, try to talk about relational reality and ecosystemic views and things like "belonging" when there is an invisible assumption of "not needing" present for many folks reading this. Take a minute and imagine that someone has embedded in their being the idea, whether they want it there or not, that they should be independent. And that person is now reading about something called "relational reality".

Now couple this with another invisible assumption: Thinking = understanding.

This invisible assumption in western culture is that because we can think a thought that we are thinking the thought accurately. We rarely question if we understand, if we have an ability to understand, if maybe we don't understand. We go right to "got it". We cannot *feel* the difference between a concept versus the lived experience that gives true understanding.

How on earth is a person who grows up in a culture of "not needing" as a value supposed to imagine or understand "relational reality" or "ecosystemic belonging?" But many people reading the words I write will assume they understand just because they follow the words. This is not an admonishment to anyone. This is not shaming. This is to say we need great humility and curiosity and a willingness to have different experiences based on whole different sets of assumptions. In other words, we need time and practice cultivating different lenses that lead to different behaviors that accumulate enough mass to counterbalance our old conditioning so that new neurological pathways can form based on whole different paradigms.

This does not happen overnight. No matter how smart or willful or awake you are - no matter how much you have processed your issues - we are physical selves and that physicality requires we work with it so new ways of being are not theoretical constructs or ideas or philosophies, but *lived reality.*

You must practice the idea that you look through lenses and that you have invisible assumptions that are so culturally accepted as to seem factual and true. This means they are invisible - i.e. very, very hard to see. And *all of us* live with them. This isn't to say they are bad. It's part of being human. Even a weird human. It's just that some of these invisible assumptions deeply antagonize Primal

Reality and our ability to live more aligned with the Deeper Intelligence. And we need to surface these things and cultivate other lenses so we can become with less stress and effort and confusion and cost of time and energy and actual money.

We begin to uncover these invisible assumptions by getting exposed to alternate ways of being, like you are, and will continue to be, in this book. We begin to uncover them by having other frameworks and lenses presented to us that we begin to utilize and then to internalize. We engage our bodies more and more and more. We cultivate humility and curiosity. And, perhaps, most importantly, we put a ton of effort into learning how to be relational.

We have not learned how to be relational, we have learned how to perform roles that allow us to navigate society as independent people who value material success and a handful of other things we are all supposed to share along with handfuls of things we are all supposed to disdain.

Take the value of "normalcy". Modern society loves the normal. Like when the doctor says "Your bloodwork all came back normal". We think normal = good. The doc thinks normal = good.

Normal actually just means a statistical norm. As in: "We took the bloodwork of 1000 people and the average, the "norm", was within these ranges. Outside of these ranges we saw measurable disease."

If you as a unique biological creature do not do well being on the lower or higher end of "normal", you are now going to begin to fall down a rabbit hole. Because now the doctor thinks you are medically fine because we make the assumption that normal=good when normal actually just equals "statistical average". A common next step would be to recommend you get psych meds like anti-depressants or something because your bloodwork indicates you are "fine", when you may, in fact, medically, physically, really and actually not be fine.

This scenario is astonishingly common. But our society values normal so much that when you are not (normal), you become kind of invisible. Because the normalcy lens does not allow people to see or think outside of it.

So you must begin to challenge your lenses. Just start to be curious. Like stop reflexively acting out a role and, instead, get genuinely curious. When someone tells you something don't just go "oh" and say whatever pat thing you might say. Say "tell me more" and see what happens. Just begin to disrupt your own grooves.

Another huge part of Becoming is to shift from the expectation that things progress in a linear manner to understand that you, and your own becoming, are, in fact, multidimensional. Let's look at this in the next chapter.

Six

METAPHYSICS OF THE SELF

Those of us in the realm of Savage Awakening are served by thinking in terms of becoming, versus "growth" or "healing". So we are not thinking in a linear way. We think of becoming as a transformation from one state of being into something else - it is a transformation rather than a progression - we are not moving "forward" or "upward", just into something different.

This is going to get a little complicated and possibly bizarre but it's crucial. So let's go a little deeper into this.

Think of yourself as a sphere with many facets, kind of like a soccer ball but with way more facets - like a chiliagon, which is like a soccer ball but with 1,000 facets. Now think of each facet as a different aspect of yourself: think in terms of your mind, emotions, spirituality, values, what tools you were given or not, what tools you have accumulated or not, how skillful you are, what capacity you have, what was modeled for you, etc. Also include every age you have ever been. And include the people and places you have been most affected by. Each of these is a facet on your chiliagon soccer ball.

Now imagine that every single person is also a chiliagon.

Now imagine that the facets can swap around all over the chiliagon that is you and all over the chiliagon that is another person and one of the things that makes these facets swap is the *interrelationship* between your chiliagon and theirs.

Read that again: One of these things that makes these facets swap, what activates these facets, is the *interrelationship* between you and them.

So imagine there is a forward facing facet that you encounter on another person's chiliagon and it "activates" one or more of your facets and those facets swing around to the front and present themselves to both you and the other person. Then the other person's facets might change their grouping and then yours might, and on and on.

Perhaps your mutual facets very quickly hit a groove and you lock into them, for good or for ill. This can cause us to perhaps hate the other person or to instantly make them our bff.

Perhaps they continually shift, making it hard to find our groove with someone. This can cause us to feel uncertain about someone or to become curious about them.

This also means that a facet you haven't seen or thought about or encountered in yourself might have been laying around on the back bottom of your chiliagon and you forgot all about it (maybe you believed it was all "healed"). Then you meet someone whose facets activate that particular facet and it migrates on up to the front and center for the whole world to see. It is also why someone you thought you knew reveals a facet of themselves you had never seen and you are thrown-off by it - because an experience they had triggered, or activated, that facet and now it's up and there to be seen.

You can verify this experience for yourself by how your behavior can change so easily, or so seemingly without your consent, when you get around a certain kind of person. Maybe you are in a good mood and you get around someone and feel "slimed". Maybe you are in a bad mood and you get around someone and now your whole day has turned around for the better just by being in their presence.

It isn't always bad. It may almost never be bad. Sometimes it can be quite amazing.

This is the nature of being multidimensional rather than linear. This is why the things you may imagine you have left "in the past" can come back up for you as if they never really went anywhere - because, in a multidimensional being, they haven't.

Please note: this is not just a singular multidimensional being in a context of independence. This is the fact of our multidimensionality existing within the truth of interrelational reality. We are affected by, and affect, the beings around us.

The implications of this are huge.

First and foremost, this more accurately models the relational nature of existence and serves to dispel notions of hyper-independence: the idea that you should be immune to others, emphasis on concepts of control, obsession with concepts of "manifesting" in the way they are most commonly prescribed, and more.

Understanding multidimensionality from a relational, or ecosystemic, perspective also greatly augments the notion of personal accountability. Where personal accountability now means being accountable for our choices and actions not just for ourselves but because we affect the well being of others whether we want to or not and whether they want us to or not.

We begin to see, and, more importantly, to accept, that there is no escaping affecting and being affected. We can only become more skillful at it. That is our job - not "control" of the self so much as accountability to ourselves and to each other. (I include non-human beings in this "each other" as well as beings many would say are not beings, like wind and fire and rocks and cars.)

We can also see that affecting and being affected isn't exclusively any one person's "fault".

All of this allows us to shift from the paradigm of not only individuality, but also of blame/guilt that our society is so addicted to.

But that's not all...

The next piece to understand is that the influence your chiliagon soccer ball self has on someone else's chiliagon soccer ball self, and vice versa, is affected by a number of variables.

The first is how rooted or not you/they are.

Another is: to what you/they are rooted.

Another is: how centered, or not you/they are.

There are more but I don't want this to get overwhelmed by complexity - I just want you to be able to work with this preliminary framework.

So how rooted you/they are...

Being rooted is a state of being anchored into something and drawing nutrients and stability from the thing you are anchored to. For example: A doctor is generally rooted into a "Medical Field" and draws stability and nutrients from this. This Medical Field, as helpful as western medicine can be, also has qualities of power-over, superiority, patient-as-stupid, knowing versus listening, and more. I'm not trying to disparage doctors. But if you have ever been on the receiving end of someone who is rooted in the medical field, you may have come away from that feeling not-too-great.

Being rooted is essential. But so is being aware of, and intentional with, what we root into. Some of us are so lost or so untethered or so lonely that we will root into anything, even if it is unhealthy for us. (We all need to root and we don't always have the luxury of awesome options when we are needing it, so go gently if you've rooted into some unhealthy things.)

This brings us to what we root into.

We humans are tiny in the scheme of things. In Feng Shui (a system of laws considered to govern spatial arrangement and orientation in relation to the flow of energy (qi), and whose favorable or unfavorable effects are taken into account when siting and designing buildings) we are tiny even in relation to the homes we live in - to such a degree that if the home's qi and our qi are not harmonious, it can affect not only our health, but every aspect of our lives! And that's just a house!

Imagine the effects archetypes, social norms and customs, families, lovers, and institutions can have on us.

We need to be rooted. But what we root into really affects what facets we live from and what facets we activate in others and what experiences we have and what experiences we simply will not be able to have.

I do not believe that many doctors who are rooted into the Medical Field are too happy to learn how truly condescending or downright damaging they are as a result. They simply, like the majority of us, have never questioned what they are rooted into.

WE NEED TO BE ROOTED. And if we cannot root into something healthy, i.e. ecosystemic orientation from a context of personal accountability, we will root into the next best alternative. Especially if it lends us the things that society values, like prestige, power, money, sex appeal, academic superiority, etc.

So we understand that we need to root. We understand that we root into something and that something may not always be super great or something we are even conscious of. Now let's look at being centered.

In modern parlance, being centered often implies being calm, cool, and collected. This is not what I mean when I use this word here.

Being centered is a quality of your awareness arising from your center, i.e. embodied intelligence, as well as pivoting around your center. Your center is your body. So being centered is living from the way your body informs your experiences.

Your body arises according to Life's Intelligence. And the more you can heal your relationship with it and center yourself firmly in it, and live from the signals and feedback and guidance it gives you, the better. This is because, at some point in the Savage Awakening experience, your body will become one of the primary tools through which Deeper Intelligence communicates with, and guides, you. Your dreams are another. But we'll touch on that a bit later.

We all pivot, or move, in this world based on what informs us. If you center your sense of yourself around anything other than your own body in a relational context, your facets will not stabilize.

Allow me to explain.

We have come to see that being multidimensional means we always have many facets, not that we lose parts of ourselves and our experiences, merely that they fall out of use/necessity/favor and we don't encounter them as much. We also have come to see that encounters with other people's facets can activate and call forth various of our own and vice versa.

We also understand that being rooted, as well as what we are rooted into, anchors certain facets in our field and makes us live from them more than other facets. And, consequently, activates particular facet responses in others according to what we are anchored into and what they are, or are not, anchored into as well. So two doctors of equal status encountering one another will likely be different than a doctor encountering a patient or a doctor encountering someone of a status perceived higher than them, like a world-renowned specialist in their field.

Where being centered comes into this is that the more centered we are, the less susceptible our facets are to outside influence AND the more consistent experiences of us other people will have. (Read that again.)

In other words, we become difficult to knock off our feet and we are basically the same person no matter who we speak with or what situation we are in. So the doctor, in this example, when they encounter us as a patient will encounter the same person as the us they might meet at a cocktail party or the same us they might meet if they encountered us as their boss. Because we are centered, we are more steady with less variation in the movement of our many facets.

We also have more of a say in which facets move to the front, i.e. get activated by others, and how much attention they get, i.e. how much they run the show, when they are activated because our facets respond to whatever has the most rooting and mass. This means the more rooted and centered you are, the more your various facets will follow your awareness and the less they will be reactive to the various things going on around them.

This is not a key to "controlling" yourself or your experiences. Outside of a relational/ecosystemic context, folks will attempt to use it to serve this purpose. Instead of controlling yourself to try to appear a certain way or have experiences you prefer, you must understand that being centered begins to lend itself to your own relationship with the Deeper Intelligence. It allows you to begin to see and experience the deeper movements of interconnection, outside of the human-created.

I want it to be super clear that being more centered and less reactive, in a truly ecosystemic reality, means we become *more responsive* to Life. We become *more* alive, more whole, more embodied. We do not neutralize ourselves.

This is because as we root more and more into ecosystemic reality that is informed by Primal Reality, and the more that Primal Reality is able to inform us through our bodies and our dreams because we are more centered, the more we are informed by the broader field of life and the less susceptible we are to the happenings within the Field of Denial in ways that are obedient to the Field of Denial. This is where we begin to experience a shift from our lives being about us into the beginning of becoming a kind of agent of Primal Reality. It's where we begin to truly transform into something else.

This is not something to imagine. You cannot until it happens. It's also not something to strive for. Again, if we are going to strive for anything it is to learn to truly be more relational - to truly experience belonging in the greater relational field. From there the Primal reality, i.e. the many beings of this world, will teach us more and more.

I know this chapter might be a bit confusing or difficult. This is going to be a really new way of considering things for a lot of folks. Please re-read it or sit with the parts you need to as much as you need to for it to wake up in you as a possibility you can begin to embody and live from. Notice what this information does in you. Just let it move around in you.

Seven

THE NECESSITY OF RELATIONSHIP

To further our exploration of the myth of independence and to deepen into relational reality, I want to speak specifically to the necessity of relationship.

The way modern society is set up, and I'm always speaking from my Western experience, is that independence is so endemic, so pervasive, so *normal*, that it is an invisible assumption that invades every single experience we have. This includes personal growth, spirituality, relationships, healing, our experiences in nature, all of it. I mean independence that exists outside of the context of ecosystemic relational being. Independence that is situated, rooted, within relational reality, within belonging, is healthy and necessary.

To understand how deeply problematic this man-made, unnatural independence is for the spiritual path, and to initiation itself, we need to understand this:

Life is in a constant state of communication and response.

The way *any* being is oriented and positioned and held in the web of existence is through the constant interaction with the life, the environment, the world in which it exists.

This means that in order to understand ourselves, to grow, and to simply exist well, we need relationship. Stated another way: We cannot grow, understand ourselves, or exist well if we are not in relationship *in a relational way.*

When we interact from a place of independence that is unhealthy and not-relational, we prevent the feedback experience that allows for our guidance, responsiveness, growth, and health.

This results in feelings of disorientation, which manifest as anxiety, control issues, and perfectionism amongst other things, as well as feeling one does not belong, feeling depressed, feeling lonely, feeling lost, feeling like one is never making headway, feeling like one is not known or understood, feeling excessively burdened, not knowing how to effectively communicate our needs and negotiate relational space, and more.

You can, per the western model, "work on yourself". You can know every single inch of your issues. You can have tools and processes up the wazoo. But NONE OF THAT can hold a candle to the relational responsiveness of life within and around us when we are rooted in belonging.

Life is a constant experience of micro and macro feedback that allows us to adjust, pivot, redirect, move closer, move away, modify, reach out, reach in, rest, inhale, explore, adventure, and listen. This relational feedback IS the thing that allows us to be at ease in what is. It is what allows the innateness of our own belonging to be felt and lived, not just thought or longed for. It is what gives us an actual physical sense of place in the web of life, where we do not have questions like "Am I here? Am I real? Is Life real?" because we are so within the thing itself that those questions cannot exist there - they are utterly irrelevant.

The Field of Denial also gives feedback. And we can too easily orient around this to get more into alignment with it. That is not hard to do with television, movies, the internet, stories, relationships, religion, much of modern spirituality and personal growth, in fact, every facet of modern life abounds with just how to do this.

So we intentionally root and center into a greater field in order to focus on, and be affected by, the proper relational information.

How a dog responds to you is information. How much flow, or not, you experience is information. The pain in your body is information. The peace you feel is information. The dreams you have, the thoughts you think, the creative urges you have, the joy you feel, the awe, the openness, the fire, the desire, the way the wind moves, all information.

We do not process this information predominantly through our heads by deciding what things mean. We process this information largely beneath consciousness, in the realm of belonging, in our bodies. We respond as a part of a larger organism, in symphony with what is needed by all, by any, in each unfolding moment. So we do not decide, for example, that "flow" means we are "doing it right", though it may certainly mean that, it is not a *rule* the way we humans try to make things rules.

This means that this information does not happen

according to a "right-action = reward" model. Do not make the mistake of making up the story that "good information", or feedback that you like, means you are doing things right and bad information, or feedback you do not like, means you are doing things wrong. The Dragon Mother is not that simple. She does not function along moral lines, she is free of taboo, and, therefore, the feedback we get is not according to what we think/believe/hope, but is according to what we learn from Life itself and from Her, or Her many emissaries, directly as it specifically relates to each one of us. We must learn to be guided.

This means that, as we believe we have learned "the rules" we immediately and vigorously shake our heads to get "the rules" out of them. Because there aren't rules - not in the way the Field of Denial implies. There is only responsiveness and the ever-unfolding moment within the physics of Primal Reality. What works in this realm is to be guided and we are guided by the things we are in relationship with. So instead of hyper-independence and seeking out rules to memorize and live by, we shift into being guided and working toward having good relationship with the world in which we live - seen and unseen, alive and not-alive, large and small.

Being guided means letting go of what we have been taught about Life and learning to learn from Life itself. This can best be done via connection with Nature. I say this because nature is often the least caustic place humans might find themselves - meaning human-created spaces have a tendency to carry tension or drama, even when they are filled with love. This means our attention is pulled from being present and we are less able to be able to truly listen.

Also, human spaces almost always reify the Field of Denial, even as they seek to be free of it. This largely has to do with the soccer ball model I outlined in an earlier chapter.

Many, many years ago, a mature cedar tree said to me "The First Lesson is to Listen".

Take this to heart. Many people do not question if they know how to listen and assume that hearing=listening.

Listening is a state of deep receptivity, humility, and openness. It is a state where we let go of the rational mind to the degree that it is no longer running the show, and we immerse ourselves in the unfolding moment however it might reveal itself.

The mind thinks first in images, so we pay attention to the images in our minds, the impressions we get, and we wonder about them. Perhaps we ask. Perhaps we offer. Perhaps we approach any being we encounter, including fire and wind and rock, with great respect. Perhaps we bend our necks and we soften and we become quiet and still and let the emergence of a moment fill us and we see what happens in this space.

By listening, by orienting to a relational context, and by being centered and rooted, we begin to experience the guidance and learning we need to be further pulled into alignment and wholeness within Primal Reality and the vast web of existence.

Do you understand the implications of this?

Your teachers are all around you! Guidance is everywhere. Belonging is as simple as orienting to the ecosystem you are already a part of and allowing it to inform how you move, think, behave, and even breathe in this world.

You must be courageous enough to act on the feedback you get. You must be courageous enough to respond to the ever-unfolding moment. You must grow your capacity for life outside of the Field of Denial. It is beautiful and terrifying, often at the same time.

You have to let go of notions of good and evil enough to discover what things actually mean and what the beings you encounter actually are. You must learn new ways of engagement. You must stop slathering Patriarchal, Christo-religious, dominator culture onto everything and figure out how to actually learn from Life what life is. You must identify, then step away from, the sock puppets in your head and the fantasies you have created that you believe are truths.

You must do this so that you can discover what life is and devote yourself to cultivating what is required to exist in it, as it is, free of the neurosis and fear that the Field of Denial instills. You will not be free of fear, or any other emotion, you will simply experience them in their honest states. This is healthy and desirable because emotions are a part of the relational nature of belonging.

The necessity of relationship means we must confront this paradox:

You do not walk the path of Initiation alone. You walk the path of Initiation alone.

When you are able to hold both of these truths at the same time without too much tension, you will be in a position to begin to truly learn and things will likely open up tremendously for you. Because you must step out of either/or thinking. You must grow beyond notions of self-as-individual and understand that the self is always, always, always relational, even when we do not see it or feel it.

The essence of the necessity of relationship is to shift from being in a parent/child relationship with the life around us and come more into respect, accountability, and mutual care. Mutual does not mean "equal". Mutual means "as we are able, we do". Sometimes we are not able. Sometimes we are abundantly able. This ebb and flow is natural.

Eight

WYRD

The Path of Initiation, indeed, of life, is better understood, and tolerated, by having a working understanding of Wyrd.

Wyrd is a Germanic concept for fate. The word "weird" is a modern descendant of Wyrd.

Wyrd is not fate so much in the sense that everything is fixed in stone and there is nothing you can do about it. It's more a way of understanding the interconnectedness of life, of the web of existence, and that everything in the web is affected by the web - that there is no escaping being affected.

Further, each of us has a set of variables that we are born with that is influenced by many things, including our ancestors. So it's not like this idea that "anything is possible". It's more that each of us has variables we can work with and the choices we make within those variables have consequences. But, still, we are bound by the variables. So it's a kind of having freedom within limits.

The way that Wyrd unfolds is moment-by-moment. It is an ever-unfolding moment. The web is being constantly woven. Wyrd is beyond our ability to comprehend. We cannot "read" it or make sense of it. It's too big and too mysterious and far too complex. There are people who can get glimpses into it. And there are certainly systems of divination that seek to extract information about it - tarot, runes, scrying - humans have many ways of peering into Wyrd, but few humans have the ability to truly access it and even this access is limited.

I very much used to be about the concept of freedom. Of absolute freedom, where "my life, my choices" ruled. I've since realized this is my feral nature, my wildness, that I was interpreting through the modern lenses available to me at the time. When I was young, concepts of "wild" were not available in any kind of accessible or sensible way. It's quite popular now to use the word wild, though it is certainly most often "wild" in the context of the FOD, which is rather bland and tame and a bit power-trippy or "glamorous" compared to the Primal Reality and the wildness one might taste there.

Freedom and independence are nearly the same thing these days. So as you negotiate your way through your own Savage Awakening process, it will help to incorporate Wyrd into your experience.

Wyrd is thought to be controlled, to be created, by three women called the Nornir. Other cultures have concepts of The Fates or of other beings that indicate an understanding of this web. They are often women and there are usually three of them. It is said that even the gods are subject to Wyrd.

You can identify Wyrd in your own life by simply thinking about it in a detective kind of way: begin to notice the patterns you have experienced in your life. It is odd if you really think about it that each one of us seems to have patterns we can identify that have been there from the beginning. In fact, the four paths of Initiation that we will talk about are ways that Wyrd plays out within the initiatory journey.

In my own life, I have had a number of patterns as early as I can recall. One is that I seem to always have intense interactions with people where we are drawn together just as they are about to go into a major transition, or while they are in a major transition. Another is one of always falling through the cracks. Like no matter how kind of smart or capable or hard-working I have been, I fall between cracks in ways where I am unsupported, invisibled, opportunities withdrawn, roadblocks appearing. Other patterns in my life are always having an urge to share knowledge and always having the urge to assist and nurture. These patterns all reveal to me clues as to my Wyrd.

What patterns do you have? What "issues" have you had to deal with over and over? What do you seem really good at? What relational themes do you have? A dear friend of mine has the Wyrd of the sacred prostitute - she just pours love into the unlovable or into spaces where love has previously not existed. She is bound by this pattern - it is her Wyrd.

When we talk about Savage Awakening, we are really talking about the Wyrd of those bound to the Dragon Mother - the patterns and experiences that those of us who belong to Her might experience. This is how I first came to notice it - via the patterns of Wyrd in my clients.

There are those of us who can access the threads of Fate. Those of us who can follow them and see what they spell. Those of us who can, if we are very careful and if we are allowed, influence the threads. I have been gifted this ability and I can tell you that one does not work with Wyrd without the permission of, and relationship with, the Nornir - or whomever your ancestry knows them as.

When I talk about relationship, I am pointing to a profound key for you. There are Spirits, Beings, behind every experience you encounter and every need you have. If you want healing, having relationship with plant spirits or with a master healer like Mengloth or one of her serving ladies, will greatly aid your efforts. If you wish to learn true sorcery, perhaps you learn how to court Kirke or Medea or Freya. If you wish to take up the runes, you may wish to turn to Odin or find one of the Jotun who will teach you differently than Odin might.

This means that the path of Initiation itself is a Wyrd path and that you cultivating right-relationship with spirit beings that have an influence or an effect on Wyrd will serve you well. This might mean a being or beings you work with who act as intercessors or who simply serve to guide and protect you so you have more wisdom as you walk and make fewer missteps either through your actions or your misinterpretations.

I have made efforts to approach the Nornir. They are not known to be warm or open to outsiders. Over a span of several years I made offerings to Them. My path eased and some things shifted, particularly threads of fate that were binding me in ways that were choking me. My path did not fundamentally change, my Wyrd is my Wyrd, but my experience of the path as I walk it has changed.

What I mean is that by gaining insight into the deeper workings of reality, and by gaining relationship with certain beings, my fear, my willfulness, and my resistance have matured and changed. I now feel more curious about They are doing with me, with how Wyrd is unfolding in my life, than in changing or fighting or trying to control what is, in truth, mine to live.

We are, all of us, subject to Wyrd. We are, all of us, bound by, and in, the web, inescapably. Cultivating the framework of Wyrd will serve you by allowing you to accept what patterns are present for you instead of fighting them or denying them. There is wisdom in this.

Modern culture tells us we create our reality and that we are gods and that we can manifest whatever we choose. The pain and suffering and delusion this creates serves none but the FOD and our own smallness. It points to our attempts to insulate ourselves, to have some space around us against the pains, which are often the result of the FOD, that we experience. It's a vicious cycle.

So we must to be curious and we also must soften into the reality of there being a kind of fate that we are all subject to. The hyper-independent self will kick and scream against this. You do not need to believe it now if there is too much resistance. Simply be open and curious about it and begin to notice patterns that you can maybe wonder about through a lens of Wyrd instead of pathology or trauma. In modern society we view pathology and trauma as requiring fixing. Fate allows us to be smart and to strategize and to take different approaches.

If you have resistance to the concept of Wyrd, you might want to follow your own belief patterns to see what need or what fear they root into so that you can understand what purpose your beliefs serve. The deeper we go on this path, the more we are required to serve Her, to serve what She requires of us, and we must relinquish what we cling to that serves our smallness. This does not mean we abandon our needs. It means we learn to meet those needs through relationship with Her in some way, not by using the methods of the FOD.

Please know that She works with what is available to us. It is not like "therapy is a FOD tool so you can't use it!" It's more that we incorporate our wyrd self into therapy and find a therapist that fits our wyrd and will serve Her agenda with us. Perhaps we do this by taking it to our altar. Perhaps we get a feeling about someone so we trust that and schedule a session with them, even if they seem hyper-conventional. Perhaps we ask a friend who also belongs to Her. There are many ways to work with this path. Again, do not invent rules. Do not make some things objectionable and some holy based on ignorant assumptions about understanding more than you do. You must earn your understanding. And this requires humility. It requires rewiring. It requires an ever-deepening relationship with Her. It requires Her favor.

When you understand that Wyrd is real, and you understand that right-relationship is essential, you can begin to see how cultivating relationship with the Unseen might make your Wyrd experience better.

We will never understand the how of Wyrd. But we can identify patterns in our tiny part of the web.

Another thing to understand on this initiatory path, because we are, to one degree or another, vessels or emissaries for Her, is that She will work through us to influence and to enact Wyrd in the lives of others.

This means you may find yourself in situations with people saying or doing things that are very much "not you" that are exactly what that person needed in that moment. We become unwitting agents of fate in a way. And it is not something we control or something we understand. Ever. We can, however, negotiate at times. Like once I was having intense PMS and just NOT in the mood to be an agent. I flat out refused but made an alternate proposal. It was accepted and I was allowed to just be me for that time. Sometimes it's not accepted and you simply must. So it is on this path.

So now we have another Wyrd pattern to notice or, at least, become curious about: What ways are you led to interact with others? Perhaps you look for the ways that directly don't benefit you or that tax you or that seem like the other person reaps gains and you are left with less-than. As agents of Fate, as emissaries of Her, we often get used in ways that do not consider the impact this has, and the toll it takes, on us.

What I mean by this is that it seems that Them of the Unseen do not understand our various situations unless we explicitly explain it to Them. Like paying rent or needing electricity and to buy food. The way we are indoctrinated, we tend to think of these beings as omnipotent. But it's like expecting your neighbor or grocery clerk to know you have a headache. They can't unless you tell them.

As you deepen in relationship with the Unseen Powers you can begin to negotiate the ways they use you. This might start by simply making Them aware that the toll is too high or that you are being harmed (being drained, depleted, emotionally hurt, etc. is a kind of harm). You can ask for different experiences or for different outcomes that include your wellness. You can ask. It doesn't mean things will change, but very often they do, especially as we are in good relationship with Them.

I have found a kind of care that comes with belonging and good relationship - I might call it love except it can lack the warmth I might associate with love. Otherwise it very much fits how love is. Personally, I am cautious about ascribing motive and sentiment to these powers. I have no idea the why of their ways. I would advise you to be cautious as well, lest the FOD sneak in and we are making Her into a kind of Jesus or patriarchal tool, thereby erasing Her and living in delusions of our own making. This is a serious, and common, risk.

You must be very deep on this path to be beyond the reach of this kind of fallacy. I know a lot of people who would consider themselves beyond this who very much are not - "powerful" folks that others ooh and ahhh over who simply have figured out how to align well with, and then benefit from, the Field of Denial. Just be genuinely, always, humble and you can avoid a lot of pitfalls.

By leaning into Wyrd, by accepting it, a different path opens up to us. Instead of trying to control reality, we partner with the unseen forces that underlie it. Instead of resisting what is, we frame it differently and see what might shift or open. I have not super enjoyed my Wyrd of being there for people during major transitions. Because it results in them moving on and me being treated quite often as if I did not just save their life but, quite the contrary, as if I did nothing at all.

I have since come to see that people want to put what is painful behind them, and to make invisible what they do not like about themselves, and I am often placed squarely in the midst of the most painful events of their lives and see them at their weakest, so they erase my contribution.

I also have come to see that hyper-independence makes us truly believe that we did the thing by ourselves - that is was really us, as individuals, that made it through, so we disappear the pivotal people without whom we could not have come through as quickly or as intact as we have. I do not feel cynical about this. It fuels me to deepen my dedication to this path and to turn every-increasingly to Her for sustenance and help. I feel grateful. Our gift and our curse are very often two sides of the same coin.

My sweetie and I were talking about this once. We were talking about how incredible it is that the things about our gifts that cause us pain can teach us so much. To this he wisely summarized: The price we pay for the gift is often a gift itself.

He said this to me one night as a commentary on his personal experience with his spiritual path and from years of observing my own. I found it profound in both its succinctness and veracity so I'm sharing it here as it may be meaningful for you.

This is only a small chapter on Wyrd. You can study Wyrd for many years before you begin to truly understand it. I would say to seek out various sources that speak about Fate, about Wyrd, and learn what you can. You may find tidbits that help. You may find cultural interpretations that speak to you. Start within your own roots. Find out how your ancestors thought of Wyrd. And do remember that the modern mind is not the ancient mind. This means that in order to understand as they understood, you must endeavor to understand them in the context of their own time and place and not assume your insights are correct or accurate.

As with all things on this path, get into right-relationship and learn from the beings around you instead of assuming because you can think, that you understand. Be humble.

For now, sit with the idea of Wyrd *as if it were true* and just notice what happens in you. What do you feel in your body? What thoughts do you have? Do you feel resistance? Relief? Anger? Grief? Tight? Cold? Warm? Hot? What do you notice? Simply explore the noticing using the practice of Be Where You Really Are and see what arises.

Nine

THE DRAGON MOTHER

Our path to the Dragon Mother is as unique as each person who walks it. Many do not "find Her" until much later in life, hidden as She is in our modern world.

The Dragon Mother is unknowable, unnameable, androgynous, in and between all things. Understanding Her is a life-time journey.

The Dragon Mother is not female or male. Because She is at the beginning and all things arise from Her, we, in our human, tiny forms, know Her as Mother. For some, She may be Father, Master, Lover. None of us, even the greatest, most profound of us, can truly conceive of Her. We may only experience Her in the glimpses, ecstasy, terror, and epiphanies we have. We may only relate to the aspects She shares at any moment She may share them.

Try to wrap your mind around Her and you will push Her away, like a child running after a ball it wants that it kicks further off every time it gets close. She morphs and changes, hides and reveals, helps and hurts. She humbles and empowers, guides and obscures, demands and nourishes.

The serpent form of Her is the earliest known form in human history. It is Her ancient form, Her Primal Revelation.

This form may actually be Her first child - a great serpent, or dragon, that she formed, that later became her lover. A great being that protects, and hides, Her. It depends on what is revealed to you and what you find.

You can only understand Her through your experiences of Her. Depending on the path you currently walk (we will talk about these paths - Black, Red, Green, White - in a bit). It also depends on what depth you reach in that path, as to the different versions of Her, different truths, you encounter.

All paths, when traversed deeply and well, lead to the same place. Those of us who have gone far enough share similar experiences of Her, whereas early on, folks might fight about what She is.

The Dragon Mother pulls us to Her through whatever systems we happen to inhabit - Hindu, Christian, Buddhist, Atheist, Agnostic, Scientism, Patriarchy, Hippy, New Age....

If we belong to Her, we cannot hide from Her or be truly lost to Her.

One of the reasons this path can be so painful is the way our conditioned self is taught to resist or fear Her, to mislabel or misapprehend or distort or revile Her. It can also be painful because She is not in plain sight in our modern culture. Many of us can feel lost and alone and this can be quite painful.

As we learn how to be in right-relationship, as we learn to move past the indoctrination of morality and taboo, we might glimpse more of Her, gain more of Her.

For many of us, once we begin to understand Her, we start to see her fingerprints all over our lives - how She has been nudging and guiding and whipping and nourishing and protecting us. Before this, most of us feel we have simply struggled too much, fallen through cracks. We do not see how our traumas and challenges have insulated us from getting taken up by the dominant culture and ensnared in the Field of Denial. We do not see that our challenges have been strengthening in us the qualities we need to walk this path.

Many people in Christian culture come to Her via Mary. Some of us explore our roots and perhaps we find Freya or the Morrigan or Kali or Kuan Yin.

If we can relax and release the need to *know* and the need to decide and land on some ultimate truth, we can be in a position to be guided ever more deeply into Her.

At some point, all of us who make it far enough down this path enter the realm of taboo. Indeed, being a pariah or reviled or scary to other humans is a phase on this path. For those on the Black and Red paths it can be especially so. But any of us who goes deep enough will begin to seem *strange* to others, no matter what we wear or how much we try to blend in.

Every single thing we encounter on this path serves the purpose of forcing us to turn ever more toward Her, to need Her more and more. We will come to experience increasing hardship when we are too far from Her and increasing ease when we are near to Her.

I caution you to not overlay Christian savior flavors onto Her. I caution you to not sink into childish notions of Mother in the way Christians do "Father" and the way modern humans do with those higher up the ladder than them.

Relationship with Her requires maturity - the kind of maturity that few adults ever achieve.

She is paradox, truth, hidden, revealed, Lover, Queen, Master, Mother.

Throughout your journey with Her, it is as if She shows you so many faces as to seem infinite in Her variations and forms. Indeed, She is.

The Dragon Mother is the Great Being who lies at the very bottom of the blackest sea.

All other spirits and deities can be known as individuals in and of themselves and also as aspects of Her. For those of us who belong to Her, it does not matter how She appears because we can always experience Her in whatever form we encounter. She has a way of both meeting us where we are at and keeping us on a razor's edge of discomfort and challenge to see Her more truly as She is.

Many people are caught up in "first" or "most real" or cultural appropriation when it comes to spiritual truths. This is understandable. But when you are on this path, She will pull you according to wisdom and whim that none of us will ever truly understand. When this is coupled with awareness of cultural appropriation, we can be mindful of our path and walk respectfully, rather than using the excuse that we were pulled by Her so we are, therefore, entitled.

The point is that we must not stop until we get to Her where She dwells, beyond the limits of the Field of Denial, beyond the limits of human cultures and times and places. We do not do this by erasing or minimizing culture, or intellectualizing human reality or discarding things because we disdain the Field of Denial - though we may disdain it immensely.

We simply keep cultivating humility and curiosity and courage and devotion, even when in the desert of faith or the Hell of Limbo. We keep making offerings, investing in right-relationship, calling out to Her, resereaching, hungering, even when we are bereft, empty, done, sick, and used-up.

The only way to know what the Dragon Mother is is to feel if you are, or might indeed be, Hers. If you feel this to be true, even as you repeatedly lose faith, lose feeling, despair, resign, feel pathetic - if that spark in you returns again and again to where you see it is the only constant, then you must go where She pulls you and not insist that it make sense or "fit" with, well, anything.

As you will see in the Three-Fold Nature of Initiation, we come closer to Her by becoming certain we have "found truth", only to leave that truth for another truth or to simply float, truthless, until we are taken up again by Her next iteration or twist.

Seriously, any spiritual encounter you have, any hardship, any joy, any shame, any taboo, any adventure, any boredom, any lapse, any shit or piss or feast or hike, She is in all and can and will use whatever She chooses to get a better hold of you. She does this by forcing you into the position to need Her because She will, at some point, become the only path you have available, the only place to turn.

As the FOD rejects you, as the majority of humans become unable to relate to you and you to them, as you become disoriented and thirsty for truth that seems impossible, you will have nowhere to go but Her. Your desperation will outweigh your conditioning and fears and you will turn, crazed and despairing, to Her. It's brilliant once you go through it a few times, but it absolutely sucks until you can see what is happening.

The idea of the Dragon Mother as it stands may not be where you are. That is okay. If you relate to initiation, if you feel something is pulling you, if you feel born to this path, She is behind it. And She may never require you to engage Her most ancient serpent form.

I am convinced that all of us called into the Ocean of Initiation know Her as the Great Serpent, or the Mother of the Great Serpent. I am not convinced we are all meant to dive into that ocean in this lifetime. Who can know Wyrd? Who can know Her reasons?

The Field of Denial, as you will learn, will use any experience we have to trick us. It will use the relationship with Her to pull a person into a power-trip or a materialism trap where they tout Her, or some version of truth, in a way that is actually self-serving but that seems powerful and true to the person in it and to those around them. This is the "false guru". This does not mean that those of us truly on this path cannot have material comfort, ease, even wealth. It simply means this territory is tricky, until you are truly kicked-out of the Field of Denial, until She truly, genuinely has a hold of you and until you have desperate, unquenchable need of Her, that you are at risk.

It might be helpful to think of the path to Her in stages: Seeker, Devotee, Adept, Sage, Vessel, Sacred Slave.

- As **The Seeker** we feel drawn, we explore, we might be "all over the map". But we are hungry for truth. This may be a phase or mature into devotion.

- **As a Devotee**, we have found a place to land that we relate to. We begin to learn some of the qualities of devotion and discipline needed. We might start to mature a bit. We try out different tools and practices - divination, altar work, meditation, prayer, dietary changes, etc.

- **The Adept** has learned the territory, gained discernment, cultivates a consistent practice of some kind, and seeks out more esoteric knowledge and tools that usually lie on the fringe of society.

- **The Sage** has matured, is usually approaching 40 or older, has life experience and spiritual maturity enough to skillfully guide others to some degree. They have deepened in their understanding, can see through to deeper patterns, and they share their knowledge with others and are recognized as a Sage of some kind, not just a knowledgeable or trained person. There is maturity, patience, intensity, compassion, and a kind of no-bullshit space around them.

- **The Vessel** is what we see in the lightest print on the map of the Four Paths in Part 3 of this book. They are called: The Black Hand, Queen's Torch, Unshakeable Companion, and Hierophant. It is where one's existence is as a vessel for how She wants to be in the world through us. As a vessel, nearly all decisions and directions on one's life are informed by one's relationship and service to Her. Her presence is felt and Her guidance and promptings are fairly clear.

- **The Sacred Slave** is what takes place in the Ocean of Initiation. This is where we not only give our lives to Her, but we undertake the radical path of transformation to become Hers in this world. We learn to navigate the Primal Reality. We have dissolved, have disappeared, and have been remade into a multiplicity. We become a form that can hold Her so that She can act upon this world through us in a way that is quite beyond the Vessel.

We become Hers in this life and the next, for all time. What we forfeit is everything. What we gain is more.

I want to speak for a moment on my reasons for titling this "Sacred Slave" as I know there will be people who will have a negative reaction to this.

We both make the choice to go toward Her as well as the reality that She pulls us. Each point of initiation involves losing increasing amounts of personal autonomy and choice. As we choose to deepen with Her, we are remade.

The uninitiated would be hard pressed to understand the transformation and benefit of belonging to Her. We do not belong to Her and retain our individual lives. No. We get pulled into the ecosystem of being and used by Her to have an effect within that system. We do this and yet are usually unable to see Her reasons or the why of what we are doing and are affecting. We are simply obedient to Her.

This is not Christian obedience or a FOD view. It is the result of the transformation of Initiation. It is the Intelligence of Life occupying more and more of us. This is what is meant by *wholeness* - it is alignment with Her, with the Great Web, with all of Life.

As we are increasingly integrated within ourselves with the Web, we change. How we see and experience the world changes, what we desire changes. We shift from self-interest to an ecosystemic orientation that is rooted in Her. Everything we begin to want is Her. The meaning we make is Her. The need we have is Her. This is where being the Sacred Slave is a limit more of language than of the self, for through this path we are liberated.

Each and every stage presented here can have experiences of being a vessel. In fact, cultivating awareness of when we are a vessel can greatly enhance our own cultivation, no matter where we are on this journey.

These stages are simply my own framework I am using to give you some orientation, some kind of guideline to use so you can see a bit about where you are and where you might be headed. May it also serve to help cultivate humility and patience.

Each place we might be will contain flavors of other places. Resist the urge to "know". Just gently hold it without gripping too hard. Otherwise you will likely create more struggle than is necessary. We already struggle enough on this path, let's not grasp so tightly that we trick ourselves, thereby extending our challenges and lessons.

As always, be humble or be humbled. For She *is* The Bender of Necks. Our work is to simply keep seeking Her. How that unfolds, none can truly know until it reveals itself, moment by moment. This is the mystery of Initiation

Part Two:

The Field of Denial and a Map of Reality

Ten

THE FIELD OF DENIAL AND MAP OF REALITY OVERVIEW

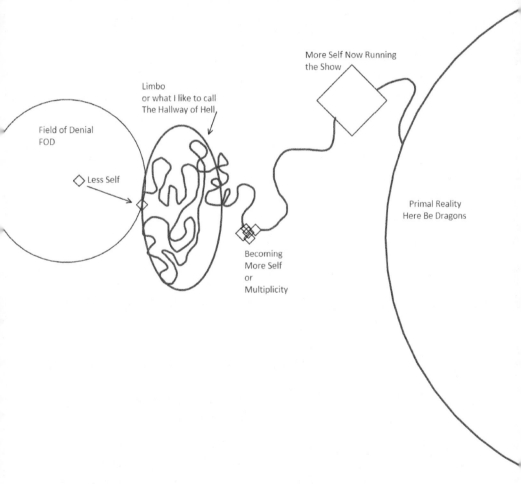

This map shows the Savage Awakening process. We start in The Field of Denial (FOD) living a false/conditioned self called the Less Self. Through often challenging circumstances, the Less Self begins to sense that all is not well in the FOD. As this awareness blossoms, the Less Self begins to seek something outside of the Field of Denial.

If the Less Self makes it to the edge of the FOD, a very intense process continues, where one begins to truly experience being "kicked out" of the Field of Denial. This is what we may call "Initiation".

If we make it free of the FOD, we land in what I call The Hallway of Hell - a limbo - where you don't belong to the FOD but you have yet to sufficiently root in Primal Reality, so you feel like you don't belong anywhere - that you have fallen through the cracks, out of place and time. This is when it is most crucial to practice rooting and centering. As you do, you will increasingly encounter the Paradox of existence.

As you encounter the Paradox of Existence, you must grow big enough to hold, and grow beyond, these paradoxes in order to further transform as you begin to find your home in the Primal Reality.

Through this process, the Less Self changes. We lose the parts that are conditioned and begin to sense more of a kind of "true" version of ourselves - what many call the "authentic self". When we get to the Hallway of Hell, the authentic self begins to lose cohesion. We experience a kind of falling out of love with our own personal experience and awaken to a profound need for something more than the "authentic self".

Our deepening need for something more than the authentic self allows us to open to relational possibilities that are unavailable to a self that is merely seeking to deepen within itself. As we open relationally, we open to ecosystemic relating, and, as we open to ecosystemic relating, we come into a felt sense of belonging.

When this happens, parts of the self begin to be replaced by a Deeper Intelligence. In this way, the individual self surrenders to the multiplicity that we actually are. This multiplicity eventually becomes a kind of no-self, what I call the More Self.

This More Self is a way of being that is more like a constant emerging, a responsiveness to the ever-unfolding of reality, where what we are depends on what the moment is in a way that is not flakey or ungrounded, but vast, fluid, and often potent. While modern western society will tend to idealize this as something to strive for, that is not the goal. The goal is to be so deeply relational that belonging anchors you. From there, who knows what might happen.

The majority of this book deals with the hardest parts of Savage Awakening, taking you to the point where your relationship with the Deeper Intelligence takes over enough that you won't need this book anymore. There will be other books that will be enriching and helpful, but you will get to a place where you are so rooted and centered that you don't need more information or "help" or, more specifically, that human help won't be all that helpful unless that human also happens to be quite strange.

Let's begin to take a look at what happens as we experience the Savage Awakening process.

We have touched on Initiation in an earlier chapter. You can be in the pull of Savage Awakening and not actually get to Initiation. There is a very delicate point in our personal growth/healing/spiritual path where we spend time and energy in what we might call "peeling back layers" or going deeper into ourselves and the unique human journey we have had.

We might learn about trauma or family systems or mental health. We might explore past lives or the enneagram or Meyers-Briggs personality types. Or we might have an event that pops open the eyes of our hearts and bellies that we cannot unpop.

What happens is that we essentially realize that what we thought life was, what we had learned it was, and what we had adapted to, was not necessarily healthy or right for us or *real*. This is when we truly begin to explore who and what we are.

In this process we are going to encounter what I call "disorientation".

Disorientation is a feeling that you have lost your way or, more often, is a state of profound confusion.

This confusion, when you do not fit in the Field of Denial, goes very deep. It is a feeling of not knowing what is going on that is so internalized you do not realize how much time and energy you spend trying to manage it.

In fact, I think the majority of what we call Anxiety Disorders are actually a state of profound, invisible disorientation.

Disorientation happens when your felt sense of how to navigate the world, of right and wrong, of connection, of what innately makes sense to you as a way to be, is not reflected and upheld in the environments you find yourself in.

For example: you see a wounded dog that is clearly homeless and clearly in pain way down the street from where you are walking. You observe maybe 50 people walk by that dog without either glancing at it or without helping it. This happens at the same time as your body sends you signals to feel concern and care for this dog that prevent you from also just walking by it without helping it if you are remotely able to do so.

This can also happen with less dramatic things, like performing social norms versus being honest. Or leading with guilt and manipulation instead of curiosity and care. It can even be as simple as a five day work week being accepted as normal when it is clearly bad for the well-being of the majority of people and their communities.

Disorientation can show up in feeling like everyone knows the rules but you. Or that everyone is okay with rules that are gross or cruel or make no sense to you.

When you do not belong to the Field of Denial, many of the rules that enable the Field of Denial to exist will seem strange, offensive, or even unholy to you.

Where the disorientation deepens is not just when your felt sense of being is out of synch with these rules, but when everyone else around you seems to be not just okay with them, but oblivious, or even thriving, with them. Including people you otherwise care for and respect.

The felt sense of this disparity creates a horribly uncomfortable tension in your body and mind and emotions. That tension feels like you are going mad or that you live in a madhouse. That tension is what I call Disorientation.

You have encountered my use of the word "rooting" many times so far. One reason rooting is so important is that it is a direct antidote to Disorientation. Without it, you are unanchored and that puts you in a terribly vulnerable position. The Field of Denial, and the folks who thrive within it, will use your disorientation against you. You will be invalidated, discredited, made to feel stupid, belittled, shamed, taken power from, manipulated, accused, preyed upon, and more.

Throughout the Savage Awakening process you will encounter Disorientation in various forms. As you attempt to leave the Field of Denial, after you have gotten out, and various points on your journey into relationship with the Deeper Intelligence of life, you will be disoriented. How it shows up for you depends on your conditioning, trauma, embodiment, and so many other things. But it will always show up. Your job is to learn to recognize it and to learn what you must do to get oriented or, at least, to not be swallowed by it.

Much of what you will learn in these pages are in service to keeping you oriented and to helping you when disorientation threatens to consume you. This whole book is, in a sense, an orientation manual. It provides you with an alternative to the Field of Denial that is relevant for us strange-souled folks.

There are many places to find orientation - many schools of thought and many tomes and teachers that say "This is the way". When you are disoriented, the idea that someone seems to know what is going on can bring great relief. And while being rescued from disorientation is a good thing, living in a framework that creates, over and over, a state of disorientation that is often so painful as to make being here unbearable, is a soul-shattering fact of the Field of Denial when you do not belong in it.

For this reason, we need to turn ever-increasingly to the relational field outside of the Field of Denial. We must practice Be Where You Really Are so that we can simply sit with the discomfort. Being able to sit with discomfort is a big part of not being so thrown off by it.

Embodiment practices, if you are not sufficiently able to access and live from your own body intelligence signals, is crucial for many people.

We need lived experiences that are different from our conformity to the Field of Denial and the Less Self to be able to change and root and center as we need to in order to move along this path. This takes time. One of the biggest challenges I see for people is the actual time it takes.

Your own becoming will take as long as it takes. You can do things to facilitate the movement, but you will not be able to know, none of us will be able to know, how long any stage of initiation will take. Particularly Limbo.

It is, therefore, incredibly important for us to manage our discomfort around time and around not knowing. We must grow our capacity to be with what is by cultivating relational awareness, embodiment, being where we really are, and our devotional rooting into this path as vessels and, eventually, servants, for Her.

Our modern minds can mightily object to what we actually are - those of us on this path find our truth, our belonging, and our safety in Her service. How that looks for each of us will be according to our Wyrd, which path we walk, and how She decides, all based in our capacities and abilities. But our devotion and practice, our altar work, our evidence journal, our offerings, our prayers and pleas and thanks, all of these things do help and we must return, again and again, to them if we are to make it through this process.

So many of us suffer over our suffering. We imagine that either we must exert more control because things are not shifting as we want or imagine they *should* be, or we collapse into our wounds of invisibility and pain, imagining we are forgotten or lost or have failed or been failed.

All of this is part of the path. And each one of us would do well to attend to how we suffer over our suffering and explore ways we may be more skillful. Ways I list above and ways I share throughout this book.

All things have a beginning, a middle, and an end. Whatever place you are in, however you feel, will change, for good or ill. You will be joyous, that will change. You will be filled with fear, that will change. We must learn to support ourselves to survive the places we find ourselves at least as much as we resist and reject and fight the places we are in. Sometimes thinking in terms of riding something out as comfortably and well as possible serves us far better than resistance.

May wisdom guide your choices and may She be around, above, and underneath you as you journey.

Eleven

THE FIELD OF DENIAL

There is so much to say about the Field of Denial - FOD for short.

First, let me say that I do not know how it began. No one does. I do, of course, have my theories.

I think the FOD arose from something I talk about in the next section on the Three-Fold Nature of Initiation - Innangard and Utangard. Since I dive into this more in the next section, I will simply say that Innangard is essentially the need we all have for a sense of safety and orderliness that insulates us from the chaos and overwhelming power of Utangard, or that which is untamed.

All humans, indeed most living beings, need a place to rest and be held away from the chaos and danger of life - from storms and fires and predators - from surviving.

I think that the FOD is a kind of out-of-control Innangard - a space humans have created to stay safe and experience orderliness - because we *need* this. But at some point it became imbalanced and took on a life of its own.

This may be because no one person had any idea what was being created and because all humans need the space of Innangard - this coupled with the unaligned ways we humans have as a result of being in bodies, ostensibly away from, cut off from, the Unseen realm. For not every human born retains connection to the Unseen realm, no matter what time period. Few, in fact, do retain connection. These people often become community healers and witches and outcasts.

So the Field of Denial grew.

I call it the Field of Denial because it is the realm where people deny *What Is.* The shape this takes depends on the culture and the time.

For modern westerners, it shows up as denying that we are in the circle of life, that we are not the center. It means denying we are integrated with life, instead of in control of it. It means denying that scary or bad things happen, no matter how hard we pray, how many affirmations we say, who we pray to. It means denying that there are things we cannot know. It means denying that there are strange and unknowable powers in this world that cannot be understood, measured, studied, or controlled through science or rationalism. It means denying that we are a multiplicity, formed and informed, by all that we encounter, utterly dependent on the web in which we belong.

I'm sure you can begin to populate the list further if you think about it. We deny that we are responsible for one another. We deny that we need outside of our own ability to self-fulfill. We deny that the earth is alive and intelligent. We deny that animals and plants are intelligent.

The Field of Denial is composed of the denials of humankind throughout our many histories. And it has likely gotten more egregious as time has gone on, or perhaps this is just how it feels to me.

Further than this, however, is that the Field of Denial, beyond just being a realm we have created, has become a kind of Being that has its own motives and intelligence. I refer to this as a RealmBeing. This realmbeing has characteristics that we can map - a kind of personality if you will.

At this point you will be benefitted by engaging the part of yourself that can engage in story by placing the "rational", conditioned mind in the background a bit. You don't need to obliterate it, but we are firmly outside its reach or necessity here.

What you want to do is to allow what you read to affect you and notice the effect it has. Then see what happens and keep going like this: engage, notice, engage, notice, engage, notice....until you land someplace solid, or perhaps just new, for a bit.

It will help if you try it on for size and just see if it seems to make some of your experiences start to make a new kind of sense. So let's dive in....

As a realmbeing, the FOD has certain characteristics.

One is that its body is composed of the people who dwell within it. It gets its power, its size, its very existence from those humans who are aligned with it and who feed into it -

the folks who are invested in its existence because they feel their own to be dependent on it.

Remember, the FOD started as that insulation we all need from the outside wild chaos. So, in a very real sense, until we have rooted into other ways of being, our lives literally *do* depend on it.

Over time, over hundreds and thousands of years, the FOD has had certain rules, or physics, that have emerged. Like power. Specifically power-over.

Whereas in the Primal Reality one would encounter predator-prey, the FOD reality has twisted this into predator and victim, specifically within the context of power-over based on personal gain that is rooted in various perversions of natural law.

An example: someone might say tribal affinity is natural for humans, so preying on those outside one's tribe is "natural". This leads to justifications for cruelty and disparity one would never find outside the FOD. Instead of "tribe" use: religion, race, neurotype, gender, social status, financial sphere, *ad nauseum*.

This is merely one tiny example.

There are, quite literally, countless examples of this that I will not go into here. What I want to do is provide you with enough of a grasp on the FOD that the ability to see it will awaken in you and you will find the patterns of it yourself. Indeed, you will begin to see it everywhere. It may be shocking. It may disgust you. It may freak you out. That's all part of this path so hang in there.

Do keep in mind that we can more clearly see the perversions in the FOD by immersing ourselves in nature and experiencing it as much as we are able. Even if you are in an apartment in a city, you can observe and engage a house plant, grass in a sidewalk, the wind and weather patterns, correlates between people and weather and stars and the moon. Listen.

As you learn from nature, as you root and center, as your innate belonging blossoms in your body, your vision and sense of things changes. Any of you reading this who have spent a significant amount of time in nature know what I am speaking of. It's just a matter of consciously cultivating what we see and learn so that we can create distinctions for ourselves that reveal the FOD in stark relief. Any way that we can do this builds and informs and assists us on our path.

I would like, here, to reiterate that a huge part of this path, and something that we will encounter over and over, possibly for the rest of our lives, is the need to break the conditioning of the FOD and also integrate the reality of being modern humans into our path. We do this not by rejecting full-stop the FOD, but by being centered and rooted in the Primal Reality by the favor and aid of the Dragon Mother. We integrate what we are and when we are and why we are with the reality of things like the FOD.

Chapter 9 is devoted to the subject of the Dragon Mother - who and what She is - and is explored and enumerated in a grossly insufficient way. This is because who and what the Dragon Mother is to you, what face she shows or what form she refuses to reveal, is a deeply personal experience for each of us. No one can know how She calls another, what that looks like, or why it might be.

Again, we must release the addiction to "knowing" so that we can learn *from* the Unseen, from life itself, from Her directly or indirectly (which is always directly though we may not see or feel or sense any part of Her).

Humans like to make up rules and morals and taboos. I don't know if it makes us feel oriented or superior or if it's just really natural and harmless. But it often happens that we do this unconsciously and then impose these "rules" on ourselves and the people around us without question and without curiosity.

Simply notice this tendency as you learn more about the FOD so that you do not create such a reactivity to it that you become ensnared in demonization or revulsion. I mean, a little revulsion is a good thing because it is fairly revulsive, but let us not orient around, and root in, the revulsion. Let us remain ever rooted and centered in Her within our own bodies as much as we are able. And let us seek out people who help us to do this when we do seek the aid of others.

Please know that She appears to us, at least initially, in whatever ways we might be touched by Her and drawn closer. So if this looks like Mary Magdalene for a time, then Freya, then Cernunnos, then Hela, then this is how it looks.

What follows is for those on the Initiatory Path and how we might experience the FOD once we awaken to it in some form. This is overly simplified so that each of us can readily grasp it in order to begin to track whatever version of this we might encounter in our own lives.

Leaving the Field of Denial is a process. Each stage of that process has its own challenges. In the version that is on the next page I just want to give you a preliminary orientation so we can then move forward. Keep in mind that the presentation of this process makes it seem like the process is linear. It's not. It's much more accurate to say it is multidimensional.

On the following page you will find a graphic of what the first part involves:

In our society we place a lot of value on the idea of "progress". We make things competitive and tend to crave feeling like we are accomplishing something. We tend to base our sense of worth on the concept of accomplishment and progress.

Savage

We kind of "wake-up" to something not being right in some way. For many we first encounter this as a "spiritual awakening" or our first move toward personal growth. This moves us away from the center of the FOD and causes us to begin seeking.

As we "do our work", we eventually encounter a kind of threshold. This is the place where most initiation that sets us on the Invisible Path takes place. Very few people proceed from here and most generally turn back, even as they think they have "gotten out" or "transcended". This is a very, very tricky place. Many people think they are at this position when they are actually just barely moved from the center of the FOD.

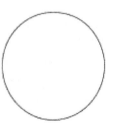

Once we are "out" we land in a kind of limbo, what I call the Hallway of Hell.

After the Hallway of Hell, we journey through the Paradox of Existence, then finally root deeply into the Primal Reality. The end result is that we live in the world as very different than how we began though it appears we didn't really "go" anywhere because most of us still participate in the social constructs of our time.

Awakening doesn't work like this, even as we inevitably bring these notions to it. This is something you will likely encounter over and over - that you are overlaying the concept of accomplishment onto the model of Savage Awakening so you can "see how you are doing" or assure yourself you "get it" or are "accomplishing" enough or prove to yourself that you are more advanced than others or that you have value..

That we care about this, even secretly, speaks more to our anxiety and the hierarchical nature of our society than it does anything else.

This is an invitation to notice - not a rule, not a thing to strive for or mimic, just a thing to have on your radar and maybe relax about a little:

Where you think you are in the above model is irrelevant.

Not because it is unimportant but because in a multidimensional lived reality, you can be any one of those places at any given moment and each one will be true for what it is when it is happening. You will be wise/you will be ignorant, you will be advanced/you will be a total beginner, you will be a master/you will be a mess.

There is nowhere to get to. Only being present to the ever-unfolding moment as you are increasingly rooting into relational reality.

Now this is where things get real.

Remember I referred to the FOD as a RealmBeing? Okay, first I want to be clear that the language I am using serves to illuminate the experience one has and how it feels. I am not striving for "factuality". Though, when you are deep enough into your initiatory path, what I am about to speak to will feel very, very real to the point of being factual.

As you wake-up to the FOD, things may feel exciting. Your eyes will open and you will discover, and be attracted to, things you never would have imagined yourself even considering. Maybe you go from being a church-going person to seeking out energy healers. Maybe you always considered yourself really rational and now you are exploring crystals and astrology. Maybe you reclaim interests and gifts and proclivities from childhood that got conditioned out of you. Maybe you feel it as a kind of permission to finally let your freak flag fly. It shows up differently for all of us.

Eventually you change enough that you confront one of your first thresholds - it usually involves making a conscious decision to leave some aspect of your FOD reality. Perhaps you quit your career or leave a relationship or move to a different state.

There will be some threshold you cross that makes it more difficult, not impossible, but difficult, to go back. For many people, this is where the Realmbeing that is the FOD begins to exert its influence.

This might show up as you beginning to have a hard time: no matter how hard you try or how much you work, you simply cannot get your head above water. It might also show up as little dangling carrots trying to tempt you back - a dream job offer your old self would have died for or the person you left getting into therapy and having their eyes opened and wanting you back with promises of a better life.

Whatever it is, there will be some variation of the FOD trying to get you to return to it. And this can be tricky, too. Like you fall in love with some wild hippie plant lover who turns out to be more motivated by money and gain than nature. Or you meet a deeply spiritual person you believe to be your soul mate only to discover they are more invested in the power that appearing spiritually advanced gives them than in actually being spiritual. There are so many iterations of this.

So you either stop here or you continue on your path.

The more you continue, the more overt will be the efforts of the FOD. It will go from trying to lure you back in to trying to stop you from continuing on to trying to harm you then on to trying to eliminate or permanently silence you.

I believe this happens because the FOD has a kind of immune system and that every person connected to the Field of Denial is informed by this immune system. They register you as belonging (to the FOD) or not. If not, they will make things difficult in both subtle and overt ways. Subtle is that they just vibe you and won't connect or be warm or helpful. Overt might be actually antagonizing you, spreading rumors, discrediting you, pathologizing you, or in other ways invalidating you *so that others will not listen to, or be influenced by you as an emissary of the Great Mother.*

I want to be very clear here that your experiences of feeling antagonized do not automatically confirm that you are on this path or that you are actually being antagonized. We need to cultivate discernment so the Less Self does not consume you.

Further, how this often works is where the Great Being that I call Dragon Mother uses whatever is happening in your life to Her advantage, so antagonizing by the FOD will be used to draw you closer to Her. This is because the FOD exists within Her realm, not outside of it. NOTHING exists outside Her realm. All is contained within Primal Reality.

You will likely find that what starts as a genuine FOD antagonism ends in the Dragon Mother getting a better hold of you.

This does not diminish the very real ass-kicking that happens. But that ass-kicking can be used by Her, and you, to deepen in your path.

As to feeling antagonized, or anything else you encounter, it is up to you to mature and cultivate discernment and personal accountability so that you can own what is yours to own. The FOD will have you using blame and guilt and shame to avoid accountability - to avoid seeing your part in the experiences you have. This is precarious territory. This is why endeavoring to understand the FOD, by noticing its patterns as we root into, and are informed by, relational ways of being is crucial. Otherwise we think we are somewhere and someone we are not and get further trapped in the FOD while being none the wiser.

The FOD does not want us to leave, as we are a kind of sustenance for it. Our alignment with it substantiates it and the more people that are in it makes it ever more difficult for it to be opposed or left.

The most common patterns I see occurring in someone's life when they are migrating away from their allegiance to the FOD are - and this is not a comprehensive list - just the most common:

- Bad luck - like feeling like you are cursed
- Not being able to get ahead
- The tools and tricks of the FOD not working for you like they do for everyone else - like you follow the steps, the rules, do the work, apply the 7 steps or whatever, and you never get the results others get
- Illness, usually chronic
- Car accidents that are not your fault - numerous ones
- Constant distractions - like just as you are about to deepen in some way on this path, a relationship or job or travel or some other enticing thing arises and you go for it only to later be let down and realize you wasted time
- Being chronically misunderstood and pathologized by those you go to for help
- Falling through the cracks as a "normal" reality
- Being invisible
- Being antagonized constantly by people and events
- Things just always being harder than they should
- Chronic financial difficulty no matter your gifts or education or abilities

- Being misinterpreted by others in ways that are actually unwell or unsafe for you, no matter how much they claim to love you or support you or "get" you

As it becomes increasingly possible for you to leave the FOD, the antagonism increases.

Something I have noticed, and that I want to put on your radar, is that this intensity ramp-up serves as a kind of training ground for us, if we take advantage of it. The hardships you face will force you, if you are determined and committed to going as far with this initiation process, and with relationship with Her, as you are able, to grow in areas that are crucial not only for leaving the FOD, but for being in service to Her and walking this path as one who belongs to Her.

Once you clear the FOD, once you make it through the Hallway of Hell, once you get comfortable with the Paradox of Existence, you may be required to deepen into the truly Strange darkness that is Her light. Here, you will be confronted with terror and confusion and joy and immensity that, without the training of this path, you will not be able to handle. I don't care who you are. All of us need to be conditioned and honed, to grow our capacity and skill and tools, for the increasing encounters we will begin to have with Her or Her agents. Just being in Her realm more directly, as one might with visions, journeys, dreams, and awake encounters, is too much for an untrained, non-conditioned human system.

So, while the FOD antagonizes us for its own ends, even this serves Her by how it hones us *for Her.* Never forget this. Always be on the lookout for the possibility that this is happening. It will help you feel less alone, though, perhaps, no less miserable at times.

The saying "Misery loves company" I think maybe doesn't necessarily have to mean that the miserable love to make others miserable, but that misery is more bearable when we are not alone in it, even as the company does not lessen the cause of the misery, still, we are helped by not being alone.

The fact that this book exists proves you are not alone in this. And though your journey may be unique, do not imagine that your suffering is more than others can imagine. All of us are pulled through the version of Hell that will most benefit and grow us. This means that each of us struggles in the ways that are the most devastating and difficult for who we are as individual people. No two of us will quite understand or relate to the very intimate terror we each will face because each of our terrors wear different faces. Let us not imagine that our pain is more. Let us not make our own suffering worse by doing such a thing to ourselves.

By the same token, let us not imagine that our power is greater or better. What She uses each of us for, what gifts She bestows, always serve Her. How, then, can any one gift be greater when all gifts serve a purpose only She can know? Perhaps you can control the weather, but what good is this to a child who needs one with the power of unfiltered innocence to be able to feel safe? Unfiltered innocence may be so unimpressive as to not seem like a power, but it can save a life just as changing the weather might. It's just less obvious. Not being able to see the truth of this power is not the limitation of the one with the power of innocence, but with the observer who lacks wisdom to truly see.

So let us, as always, cultivate humility. For none of us truly know Her ways or reasons. And all of us who serve Her are equal in usefulness because of Her skill, not because of our individual powers or aptitudes or depth or intelligence or spiritualness. Let us never forget this so we do not give the FOD openings and make our spirits food for it.

Twelve

LIMBO or THE HALLWAY OF HELL

We have established that the path of Initiation is not linear. So "making it" to the Hallway of Hell does not mean you won't still contend with the FOD. We will probably always contend with the FOD in some way. It is, after all, a part of us, like it or not. Our bodies were made and grown in it.

One can feel they encounter limbo many times. Throughout the initiatory process we will encounter pauses, rest periods, and feelings of waiting that are more akin to gestation. This is not Limbo. The first true Limbo is markedly different from this.

The first true Limbo has a quality of truly being "kicked out". Though our relationship to it, and it to us, will morph and change, the first true Limbo is often the most severe. This is primarily because of the ways we change.

If we make it through the first Limbo, successive ones will feel more like gestations. My theory is that if you do not make it through the first Limbo, and you do return to the FOD without losing the gift of Initiation, that you will encounter another Limbo much like the first. Though I have not personally met someone who entered Limbo and chose to return to the FOD, that did not then have their Initiatory link with the Great Mother severed. This does not mean it doesn't happen, or that it's not common, simply that I have not encountered this in the people I have worked with. Perhaps our paths diverged and it's simply that I never knew what became of them.

Limbo is just that: an uncertain period of waiting. On the initiatory path, it can truly feel like you fell into some kind of bubble in a void, where you do not belong anywhere anymore. The feeling of having been kicked out - of society, of life, of human reality - is palpable and pervasive.

Feeling you do not belong anywhere is a defining characteristic of Limbo. This means that you don't so much feel like an outsider as it feels like no matter where you are, things do not make sense like they used to, things do not work for you like they used to, and your sense of purpose, if you had one, will evaporate or, in some cases, erupt so fiercely as to be undeniable and all-consuming.

When we enter the limbo of initiation, it is where we begin to unravel. The Less Self begins to truly lose cohesion. The reason this is so uncomfortable is not just that we are "losing" what we were, but that we have not yet become what we are to become and we have no way of figuring out what even that might be. None. Zip. Zilch. Zero. It's like everything we thought we knew and were and had figured out suddenly is just...gone.

Limbo is a place with no footholds, no finger holds, nothing to grasp or name or compare ourselves to in any way that might be clarifying. We simply know we are no longer what we were. And we feel...forgotten.

In limbo, especially in the beginning, we yearn for structure, for purpose, for clues and hints and notions about what we now are. In limbo, there are none.

Limbo makes it so you cannot turn to the FOD for help or comfort. It makes it so that the people you talk with, seek for help, the people you *need,* will only push you further from the reality you are no longer aligned with. You will grasp desperately at what used to work, what used to help, only to find yourself helpless and nowhere.

You cannot explain it because everyone you tell will think you have some issue to resolve or some purpose you must find or some mental illness. They will not rejoice and laugh and congratulate you. I mean, I do when I encounter people in limbo, but no one in limbo appreciates the congratulations until they've gotten through the first bits and have gotten some glimpses of light coming in - little peeks of insight or a new view.

Limbo is not only a state of unbecoming, it is being put in a place *where you have nowhere to go but towards Her.*

Its purpose, so far as the human being is concerned, is to force us to turn to things, to open to things, we literally would not be able to open to and turn toward if any human help remained for us.

Limbo puts us in a place where we become so desperate as to consider that perhaps the Unseen realm is real. Perhaps Unseen beings are real. Perhaps one might try an altar practice and giving offerings to invisible beings and see what happens. We become desperate for help.

"Desperate Need" is a quality of those devoted to Her. It is a normal and necessary part of this relationship. Desperate need anchors us to Her when we would otherwise drift or perish.

All of Life has a desperate need for the Mother. It is simply that the FOD has denied this to an unfathomably egregious degree. Limbo awakens us to the fact of this need. And, if we are fortunate, it bends our necks enough that we never forget it. If we are truly lucky, our desperate need blossoms and fills us so that we never stray from Her again.

This is a huge gateway in the initiatory process.

Limbo is where those who are truly meant for this path finally find their feet firmly beginning to root to it and where those who are not meant for this path return to the FOD but in what I call a "pocket realm".

Let me briefly address this "pocket realm".

A pocket realm is what I call the various little realities that form inside of the FOD. Many of these pocket realities are created by/with/for people who believe they have left the FOD but have simply upgraded or transformed the way they function within it and cannot tell. I do not mean to be condescending or disparaging of people's paths and efforts here. If anything, this should illuminate a couple of things:

One is how genuinely tricksy the FOD is. For all of us. The other is that this points to how essential humility and willingness to not-know and curiosity and right-relationship are, for without these we can think we have gotten someplace, or done things, we actually haven't. Enlightenment is a good example. Power is another. So many people truly believe they are enlightened or powerful when they truly are not. For both the enlightenment and the power serve the hierarchy of the FOD. That's all.

To be fair, I think that the FOD is so genuinely not-magical that any tiny bit of magic seems like A LOT. It is so not-conscious that any tiny bit of consciousness seems like A LOT. It is so filled with rationalism and scientism and moralism that any phenomenon of the Unseen realm seems freaky and WOW. So when people firmly in the FOD experience any of these things, it can be easy to distort scale because the distance between nothing and a tiny bit of something, in FOD context, seems gargantuan because we have absolutely no idea how deep the possibilities are *because we have not become the people who can experience them*. So people in the FOD are like "You have zero and I have .75! Point seven five!! Do you have any idea how rad I am?!!"

The FOD thrives on distraction. And this scale distortion, as well as the fall-out from it, is a major, often life-long distraction that serves as a net, or illusion, people cannot tell they are caught in.

This is why we invest in right-relationship. This is why relationship is necessary. Because we *cannot*, by ourselves, truly tell where we are and the FOD will absolutely distort our lenses to make us believe we have left/transcended/gone beyond it. We cannot tell how great or small the magic we experience is.

This is not to say that magic must be great to be real. Not at all. It is to say that the context in which we experience things, the broader reality we engage in that informs our experiences, absolutely makes a difference as to the effect the experiences have on us. To simplify, it is not what you do but the field in which you do it that matters. Because the FOD will use your experiences to pin you down in it and it is very, very hard to tell it has done so.

Because pocket realities.

Pocket realities are like little mini-FOD's. They can even have metaphysics that conform to the beliefs that compose the pocket reality. Like a Law of Attraction pocket reality will absolutely have metaphysics that conform to the Law of Attraction, just enough that it is substantiated, but not so much that it is actually true for everyone. This is where hierarchy comes in and power trips blossom and then the FOD infiltrates with all its little nuggets and then you have a Law of Attraction flavored fractal of the FOD.

All pocket realities are like this. And because the FOD exists within Primal Reality, Primal Reality is also experienced there. You can now see how easily one gets trapped in this, right?

So Limbo is most often experienced after one has already been in many pocket realities. One must experience a number of these to begin to *feel* truth versus not-truth in one's own body - where the mind and the FOD and other people who are invested in the pocket reality cannot dissuade or trick you because you are literally, physically being informed by the greater realm in which you have been rooting.

The shortest time I think I have ever seen someone in true limbo is two years. The longest is nine. This is not to say this is how it is. I have not met every person on this path, not even close. I'm just wanting to give you some idea of what it might look like for you. You could be in for one year or twenty. I do not know. But I do think 2-9 years is kind of fair as a ballpark. Just don't get fixated on that.

Limbo is a non-place that the Less Self cannot stand. Because it means the Less Self's destruction or, more accurately, its subsumption. But the Less Self can only interpret this as destruction.

You can begin to see why being centered and rooted is so important. You can begin to see why relationship is essential. You can begin to see why getting out of knowing will serve you well. All these things are essential to the transformational becoming of this path. And it will make Limbo something you can survive without retreating back to a pocket realm within the FOD, or just FOD straight-up.

Going through Limbo means you MUST allow the unbecoming, the unraveling, the destruction, to happen. You will not be able to allow this if you do not become utterly, desperately, wholly dependent on Her. Your desperate need must be drenched in devotion so that roots into Her may grow. Otherwise you will just have another wild experience that is not really anything but a fancy light show and you won't gain or grow the way true initiation requires.

Many factors affect our experience of limbo. There is no right or wrong way to do it. There is no good or bad way to do it. There is only your way of doing it.

One thing I will add here is that people who are born to this path who never truly get diverted from it tend to have a shorter or richer limbo. Those who were born to this path who were diverted from it often experience a more empty, longer limbo. All Limbo experiences suck. But sucking when you know it's getting you somewhere eventually versus sucking with no end in sight is the difference between Limbo and true Hell.

Those of us born to this path and diverted from it do not have the same lived experience of knowing and connection to Her as those of us born to this path and not diverted from it. (Dear All-Things-That-Are-Holy, please do not turn what you just read into a power-trip or some kind of measuring stick)

If you are truly in limbo, it _is_ leading somewhere, and the unraveling it brings will be the greatest blessing you have, up to this point in your life, ever received. Because what it makes possible for us is beyond words or imagining.

Everything in this book is in service to you navigating this path, including Limbo. If you are, as you are reading this, in Limbo, then rejoice, for you now have tools to practice that will genuinely help you survive it.

Thirteen

THE PARADOX OF EXISTENCE

A **Paradox** is a situation, person, or thing that combines contradictory features or qualities.[1]

Examples of paradox:

- Life/Death
- Sacred Rage
- Helpful Torment
- Being Broken Creates Strength
- Dissolving to Become Whole
- Great Power in Humble Places
- Freedom and Accountability
- Healer as Predator

The above examples are all paradoxes that you will encounter on this path. There are many more than these.

On this path, the Paradox of Existence is something you must grow your capacity for. Because it means integrating what life is. It means releasing ideas and beliefs and conditioning that deny these truths.

As with most things on this path, you will encounter

---

[1] From dictionary.com

paradox over and over and over as you go through whatever stage you are in along the lines of what I spoke of earlier about the gentle ways we are conditioned to be able to face what lies ahead. When you might reach the Paradox of Existence, however, is only after you have truly made it through Limbo.

This is because Limbo unravels us enough for the wholeness of life to appear to us as it is, unfractured, undissected, as non-opposites. When we have truly made it through Limbo, the opposites of life - the choices, the distinctions, the differences, the appearance of this-or-that, all appear as a kind of illusion, and the previous weightiness of decisions begins to evaporate because we begin to see, arising from the evaporating mist of duality, Her. And we now understand that all we must do is follow Her.

She begins to truly reveal Herself as we are truly able to apprehend Her. This happens when the encounter with Paradox no longer creates tension within us.

Let's take Life/Death for example. Many people experience these as opposites states. Life and Death are the same thing. They are the various representations of one thing. If you truly understand Life, and you truly understand Death, you will see that these are only guises of one thing. Not because of some philosophicalized optimism slathered onto Death - like "life comes from death" or "no one ever truly dies".

No.

When we encounter the Paradox of Existence, after we have genuinely gone through Limbo, we are required to see and experience what Life is without tension, without need to change it, without wrestling. Just to be in it. Limbo makes this possible.

The unraveling that happens in Limbo clears out enough of the Less Self that, as we root even more into the Primal Reality and move closer to Her with our desperate need, we become more like Her. And She *is* Paradox. She is also more. And She is also not Paradox.

This is not where I explain to you what paradox on the initiatory path is like so you can construct some idea about it in your head. That serves none but the FOD and the neurosis of the Less Self. You will not be able to grasp this with your mind. And if you think you understand but have yet to be destroyed, dissolved, have yet to hunger with unquenchable desperate need for Her, it is all ideas, puffs of air.

Here, I am putting it on your radar that the Paradox of Existence *must* be encountered and resolved in such a way that you not only feel no tension with it, but find it utterly beautiful, awe-inducing, and it drops you to your knees. The Paradox of Existence is where true devotion arises in us as natural, and as essential, as air, for, once awoken, we can never be without it.

Traversing the Field of Paradox, from an Initiatory Path, is like walking within Her body. She is everywhere, all at once, inescapable, perfect, terrifying, unfathomably complex, vast, and so intimate as to be inside the very spaces within you. The tension you have held about life, your fear, your vulnerability, your smallness, relaxes and you no longer experience your fear and vulnerability and smallness as awful. The pain of what we are is still there, but it floats in the Ocean of Her and means something vastly different than it means to the part of us that cannot hold its perfection because we could only experience it as fractured.

If Limbo is where we dissolve, the Paradox of Existence is where we begin to become whole[2]. We begin to become a multiplicity even as we are one being. We embody the paradox that *is* Primal Reality. Our literal being comes to exist outside the tension of Paradox and we experience that we are holy.

---

[2] By whole I mean "unity", not "unbroken".

Fourteen

PRIMAL REALITY

Primal Reality is the original, ancient, essential field of reality. Speaking about it is nigh impossible because it is everywhere. It is also the body of reality where we most directly experience the Dragon Mother.

Because all reality exists within the Primal, our experience of it depends more on where we are than on it, per se.

Many people don't ever notice it. Others only experience it via nature.

Because Primal Reality is not governed by the Field of Denial, the FOD conditions us to be at odds with it - to disdain or reject it.

Primal Reality is not moral. It does not function on good and evil. It is savage, yes, but it also has laws. Primal Reality is ecosystemic and relational, it is also cold and removed. Coming through a true experience of the Paradox of Existence prepares us for this, and we are able to engage this far differently than the Less Self can. The Less Self is freaked out by Primal Reality.

What we experience of Primal Reality and how well we get to know it depends, for the purposes of this path, on our relationship with Her. Regardless of whether or not you are on a path of initiation, Primal Reality can be experienced to some degree based on one's interest, openness, and time spent in direct contact with the land.

The land teaches us. Each of our ancestors at one point learned from, and was informed by, the land. Our bodies are made of the land. The various places we might live teach us the wisdom of that specific place and also reveal deeper insights into the nature of Primal Reality.

Primal Reality is available to all, yes.

But on an initiatory path of the Dragon Mother, the Primal *is* Her.

As we deepen in connection and devotion with Her, we experience the beauty and ferocity and coldness and belonging of the vast web of existence.

To truly meet the Primal we must leave the Innangard - the safe and orderly places we create and seek (we will talk about this more in the next chapter). This does not mean that we are unprotected. As you will learn in the next chapter, if you go into the Ocean of Initiation, you leave the safety and comfort of Innangard. The only way this happens is by learning to work with the beings of the Primal to keep you safe in the Primal.

Direct encounters with the Primal are not something we should seek, for they usually are experiences that can, and do, kill us. Like the photographer who was eaten by a bear he had been visiting and photographing in the wild for years. Or the wild river that drowns the one who has rafted down it countless times.

When we enter the Primal by leaving Innangard, no matter how protected we try to be, going into the wild and ancient realms always carries the possibility of harm or death.

If you are called into the deepest waters of initiation, that is, if you are called to become Her servant and vessel in this world, you will need to go into the Primal by leaving the Innangard - a journey few humans ever take.

As I have said in numerous places and in numerous ways, going into the Ocean of Initiation is not a power trip or a thing to desire because of our ideas about it being somehow cool or better-than. It is a fool's errand to do so unless you are explicitly pulled by Her.

You can definitely pursue it. You can dip your toes in the dark waters of it to get tastes. But you will not survive without her favor and aid.

What dwells in the Primal would terrify most humans. Terrify or drive them mad. This is not hyperbole.

Our conditioning would view the beings of the Primal, as well as its laws, with horror and revulsion. What is required of us to go there, many would find repugnant or unimaginable.

I am not going to elaborate on this here by giving any examples because, if you are required by Her to enter, She will guide you. If you are not, it will just be an indulgence of morbid curiosity and I will not profane Her or this path like that.

As I have said from the beginning - this path is not linear and there is no "end". There is only the place you and She get to.

I would not wish being required to go into the Primal on anyone. But for those of us required to enter, it is the most profound thing we could do with our lives. Because the end of this path, the true end, is that we are so transformed as to exist for Her, because of Her, as Her, forever, and that we want only this, no matter the cost.

If that freaks you out or makes you feel despondent, Be Where You Really Are and maybe explore the possibility that this is not for you right now and leave it be.

Part Three:

The Three Fold Nature of Initiation

Fifteen

THE THREE-FOLD NATURE OF INITIATION OVERVIEW

Initiation has three qualities that all work together to lead us to what we are to be: The Call, The Pull, and Metamorphosis.

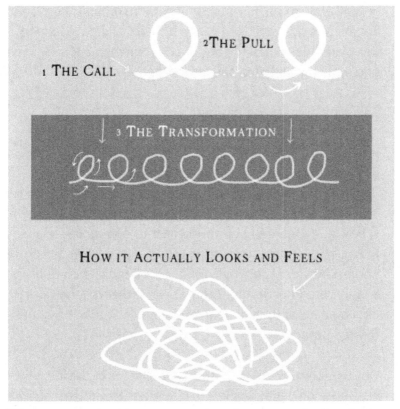

When we are in this process, one time around often feels

so profound, i.e. one time of experiencing call → pull → metamorphosis, that you feel like you're done - you're now where you need to be. The truth is, this process happens over and over and over, possibly for the rest of your life.

The value around "knowing" in our society can make this process more stressful, or misleading, than it needs to be. I invite you to really dig down and commit to the practice of curiosity and the practice of cultivating relationship with the Unseen Powers - whether that is ancestors, land spirits, familiars, or others.

In fact, every time you assume your turn around the loop of initiation is over and you "made it there" and have landed in the place you will now stay, catch yourself. Catch yourself and remind yourself of these words:

There is no "there" on this path.

When you belong to the Dragon Mother, initiation is perpetual, even as you need a break from initiation.

The path of initiation is one of having something stir in you (The Call), then gaining an interest in something in a way that just takes you up into it (The Pull), then going down some kind of rabbit hell (instead of rabbit hole - if you know, you know) and then feeling the requirement to change and/or being bent and broken into new shapes (Metamorphosis).

Our tendency to value "progress" drives us to decide where we are on the scale of human enlightenment or consciousness or power. The Dragon Mother is the

Bender-of-Necks. She will humble you like a huge, cold, relentless hammer until your ideas of you having power or being "all that" are beaten out of you. Consider this your heads-up - do with it what you will.

In the process of this Initiatory cycle, one of the things that I see quite often is that someone goes through "call - pull - metamorphosis" in a way where they are humiliated or degraded or canceled only to regroup and come back with "I'm more powerful than you knew!" and kind of double-down on their Less Self cluster, fancying that they are now somewhere "beyond" the rest of us schmucks.

There can be a feeling of having your eyes opened, which they may be, but this, coupled with the unbending neck, i.e. lack of genuine humility that is required, means a person steps into more arrogance and deepens in their ignorance because they truly believe they are somewhere and that this somewhere is somehow beyond or above most other people. While this may be true, it is true predominantly in the context of those people enmeshed in the Field of Denial.

What happens is that someone encounters a Power Pocket within the Field of Denial and buys into it, thinking themselves as having gone beyond the Field of Denial when, in fact, they are at risk of becoming even more ensnared. I call this "crawling up your own arse". We've all done it, or we're all going to do it - it's just part of the ride.

Instead of the addiction-anxiety to progress and how advanced or aware or enlightened or powerful or in-the-know you are, commit to cultivating the only pursuit that matters, and that is our transformation into being Her hands and heart in this world. What that will look like depends on your Wyrd and how you cultivate relationship with Her and how devoted you are. Note: relationship and devotion are not places for ego, so this shift in focus will serve you well.

You may actually have the experience of getting closer to Her than any mortal on this planet, where you gain favor and powers beyond comprehension, and you find yourself living in a little shed somewhere feeding someone else's chickens with no internet and no book deal and no one cares who you are. Those chickens will be the most blessed people on this planet if that happens. But chickens aren't exactly held in high esteem in the FOD. Yet, there you are, all wise and with the chickens.

The point is, none of us knows where we will be. So long as She is our main focus, things will unfold for you.

If you are walking this path to fulfill your unmet human needs in a human framework, consciously or unconsciously, this path will give you the opportunity to confront your secret desire to be acknowledged as powerful or worthy or whatever it is. Not by the attaining of power, but by having your powerful little face shoved in cold, wet manure over and over and over until you give up chasing such things. This is, of course, if you prove worthy of Her. I have found She tends to give those of us who belong to Her many, many opportunities to bend our necks.

You have power because She chooses, because you earn it. You do not have power because the people in the Field of Denial throw money or fame or oohs and aaahs at you. And what most people decide about having earned power, therefore deciding their power is real, haven't even scratched the surface of this path.

The Island of Initiation and the Ocean of Initiation

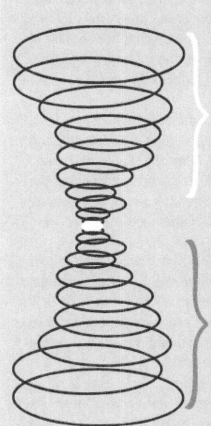

The top spiral is the Island of Initiation. Here we have many "Shadow" experiences and little glimpses of the Underworld we tend to call "Dark night of the soul". Because this Island Initiation is so intense, many mistake this for the whole of Initiation. This is generally accompanied by feelings of knowing more than others, of having unlocked profound secrets only the Initiate truly gets, of thinking one's teachers haven't "gotten it" as much as oneself has, and feeling you understand "the Underworld" and "shadow" and "The Dark Mother" because you have been through some things. This is where we are unravelled and remade over and over, each time thinking we've arrived. This is the Initiation of the Upper that prepares us to go into the Darkest Light.

The bottom spiral is the Ocean of Initiation. This is where the Great Mother, the Red Serpent, the being that is nameless, formless, and unknowable, begins to be truly reveal herself. This is where the requirement for true devotion and the utter remaking of those that belong to Her happens. You thought things were weird and potent on the Island - you thought you were in the power then. You were feasting on crumbs. The Ocean of Initiation is the realm beyond words - the realm of being that has no translation. You must experience this yourself. The powers you encounter here are truly Life and Death. This is where Black Hand, Queen's Torch, Unshakeable Companion, and Heirophant coalesce, fade, and She truly steps through us into this world.

=

This graphic shows the Journey of Initiation. We start at

the top, in the Island of Initiation, entering with The Call. If we answer the Call, if we follow it, we must make a great deal of effort. Then the Pull takes over. Then we begin to go through Metamorphosis that takes us deeper and deeper into the realm of Initiation.

As we descend, our path gets more specific, we discover or cultivate powers, we begin to see the world differently. Here we encounter the increasing need to practice right-relationship with beings of the Unseen Realm. This is where we practice and experiment and theorize and have numerous bizarre, difficult, wonderful experiences.

This upper Island is where questions of sanity, job loss, relationship changes, crisis, humiliation, power trips, and the general migrating away from the Field of Denial, navigation of the Hallway of Hell, and confronting the Paradox of existence happens. In other words, the majority of the map all takes place in this upper field.

Many people will naturally think that leaving the Field of Denial means they have made it to the Ocean of Initiation. Or certainly when one makes it out of the Hallway of Hell. After all, the experiences have been so powerful, we have seen so much, we have become so different, so weird, that surely we must be so far progressed.

Again, cultivate the awareness to notice your need for progress and power. Then turn away from this and turn toward relationship with the Unseen. Turn to it over and over and over and ask these beings to help you and guide you. Turn toward this until the need to turn to it is gone and you simply dwell here without tension. This is not something most who walk this path will do and they will turn back to the FOD or hunker down where they are and make what they can of it. This is why we go around and around and around - so the many layers of conditioning can shift and the many ways that we need to transform can happen. We must address the anxiety and fear this elicits or it will be our undoing.

I want to address something crucial about Initiation and about humans in general: we need safe places, orderly places, non-wild places, for our wellness.

To ancient Norse peoples, this was expressed as Innangard and Utangard. A place is Innangard if it is orderly, civilized, and law-abiding. Utangard is wild, chaotic, and "lawless".

You know the white picket fence? This originally was a way to establish Innangard around one's home. The fence does nothing physically "protective" - it simply delineates the space between the tamed and the wild. *Because we need this*.

The Island of Initiation, as wild as it may seem, happens largely within a kind of Innangard. In fact, much of the Initiation of the Dragon Mother is helping us transition from Innangard to Utangard by teaching us what we need in order to be safe in the Primal - in the realm that is Utangard.

When we get into the Ocean of Initiation, Innangard is not available to us. We do not bring lawfulness and order and non-wildness to this place. What we must do in the Ocean of Initiation is learn to work with the reality of the primal to stay safe within it. This means working with ferocious spirits to keep us safe from other equally ferocious spirits that would harm us. This means making pacts and bonds with beings more potent than we are. And, ultimately, this means transforming into something of the Primal - becoming something that is at home, and welcome, in Utangard.

This is why, when people talk about initiation, they are talking from within Innangard, feeling themselves to be wild though they need Innnagard to survive. Very few humans transform enough to have a genuine encounter with Primal Reality - the substance of Her body that is the most gnarly and frightening and savage place of existence. We cannot dwell solely there in human form, but we can transform enough in this life to encounter the Primal, not by defending ourselves against it with the rules and order of Innangard, but by learning to work with Utangard itself.

There is no book you read on this which will explain it. There are, however, books you can find that will show you how to earn the abilities needed to survive, or, at least, enter. These are not for the faint of heart. And not something you should associate with "progress". You must truly be *of Her*, you must truly transform into a creature that is something other than human while you are in human form. The implications of this, I hope, are not lost on you. To live in this starkly Innangard reality - the Field of Denial is the ultimate Innangard - and to become a creature that can walk in the Primal is a dangerous, difficult, and life-long path.

The upper realm of initiation is still going to be gnarly. You will still gain power, abilities, and incredible experiences by dedicating yourself to it. You will spend decades in it. Your goal should not be to go into the Ocean of Initiation unless you are sufficiently changed and absolutely certain you belong to Her and want nothing more, nothing else, than this with your life.

Do not let the power trip of the human-created drive you to the depths. Your sole reason for even thinking about the Ocean of Initiation is to belong utterly to the Dragon Mother. Until you have been through many rounds of initiation, it is impossible to understand what it means to even consider this. Again, this is no place for your wounds around power, recognition, etc. This territory is dangerous, not glamorous.

Hopefully you understand that the Island of Initiation is worthy, rich, transformative, and can provide a life-time of powerful transformation and experiences. It is a noble pursuit and worthy of a lifetime of dedication. I am not meaning to put anyone off this path. I am meaning to be very real about what it is and to break through the illusions of the FOD and the illusions of the Less Self that will crave the idea of the Ocean of Initiation. Those of you that have the Wyrd to make it to the Ocean of Initiation are also being given some idea of how deep this path can go.

Now let's look more in-depth at each of the three aspects of the process of initiation then we will go on to explore the Four Paths of Initiation.

Sixteen

THE CALL

For many of us, The Call is unnoticeable at first. It's something we won't even be able to see until we look back from having already gone through initiations to see how long we have been sung to by Her.

The Call can show up in a lot of ways, depending on where you happen to be. You can think of this as a "wake-up call" - where something happens that shakes you out of the trance of normal life. For me, this was a moment of piercing insight I had at seven years old that revealed the FOD to me. It was so potent that I took a vow to this path at that age. For you, it may have been a near-death experience, a trauma, a potent spiritual experience, or something like an increasing feeling of not-belonging or numbness or disillusionment that becomes so consuming that you realize you need to seek help.

The Call can also be like a repeating theme that you ignore until you can't ignore it anymore. Like a client of mine who belonged to a major religious group but who always felt very connected to Eros, or erotic energy, that was simply NOT allowed in their culture. They began to explore the fringes of that energy in ways that were "allowed", like art and theater and singing and also via "working on themselves" in therapy and other ways.

They finally were put in a position where they could no longer ignore the truth of themselves and left their church. That was one kind of metamorphosis. Once that settled, more Calls came in, along with more requirement for change.

In the Field of Denial, The Call reveals itself by us waking up to the fact that our way of being is not working for us. It can really open a can of worms.

The Call often, not always, but often, starts very gently. Meaning it isn't some big WHACK! we get.The Call then gets increasingly loud and hard to ignore each time we do not answer it. This increasingly loud nature of The Call comes with increasingly costly consequences of ignoring it. Maybe we know we "should" go to therapy because we think we might have a little baggage from growing up with a narcissistic alcoholic but we think we're mostly fine so we don't. The anxiety we carry from this begins to reveal itself more and more.

This then increases. Maybe we have an actual panic attack. Once it passes, we ignore it or forget about it, thinking it was a fluke. Until we start having them multiple times a week and now are so inconvenienced by them as to be unable to continue normally and we are, essentially, forced to address it.

This is the nature of The Call. You will not be allowed to ignore it. Not if you are on this path. You just won't. The Call will get louder and harder to ignore until you are forced to deal with it. Being the resilient, stubborn creatures we are, this often means getting very ill or breaking a leg or

138

losing our livelihood or losing our friends or almost dying before we finally relent and pay attention.

But how cool is it that we have something there that is not letting us just exist in a life that doesn't truly work for us? That we have something walking with us, invisibly, that won't let us get completely lost down wrong paths?

Each time you go through a cycle of initiation, the next one will start with a call. Once you go through a few, you will start to recognize The Call for what it is and respond to it before it gets too loud and the consequences get too costly. At least, I hope you will.

One final thing about the call:

You may have theme-clusters to yours. What I mean is that when you first start getting called, it may be in the personal growth arena, or the health arena, or the crisis arena, or the relationship arena, or the livelihood arena, or the spiritual arena, or any other arena that there might be for a modern person.

Your first few rounds of initiation will generally all have the same theme of a call. This is because you will need several rounds to sufficiently shift around a particular theme that has a hold of you. If you grew up in an unhealthy household with childhood trauma, your theme might be personal growth/psychology and things dealing with the mind.

After you "finish" this cluster you kind of graduate. And this graduation is often into a new theme that is the next step of the old theme. Like you go from psychological themes requiring personal growth into physical themes where you learn you haven't been in your body because of your trauma. You thought dealing with psychology was enough. You learn in your next cluster that dealing with your body is essential and that you need to be very embodied to be healthy and to be on this path.

Each theme cluster leads us to another theme cluster. Some theme clusters can be very short, just a round or two of initiation cycles. Others can take a decade or more.

And because this path isn't strictly linear and because Her requirements of us are so intense, you will not be allowed to trick yourself! Isn't that cool? I mean, it's terrible, but it's also really cool.

How this looks is this: You work on the theme cluster of psychology. This leads to awareness of more alternative approaches, some of which light you up in surprising ways. Or you meet someone in that theme cluster who introduces you to something you need that you wouldn't have found had you not been in that theme cluster.

Then you spend a decade or more working on yourself and get your psychology dialed to the point you could have a PhD in psychology, you counsel friends, you help others, etc. You think you've really "dealt with your shit".

Then you get sick. Like you feel unwell, fatigued, aching, can't sleep. Doctors can't figure out what's wrong. They think it's psychological but you know you are all dialed on the psychology. So you get into nutrition and herbs and the whole rabbit hole of health. Then you find connections between the body and the mind and you have a new perspective on yourself. You look deeper and you look in a new way that is different than the way you looked when you were in your psychology cluster.

You are also so "seasoned" at working on yourself that the capacity and skills you have developed allow you to get to deeper insights more quickly and you have less tolerance for your own bs and that of others.

You discover there is something in you you have been ignoring. It's been there your whole life and it wants attention. It's not psychological. It's not physical. But had you not gotten sick you wouldn't have found it because you thought you were fine. And had you not gone though your psychology cluster, you wouldn't have been able to see it.

Maybe it's a buried talent? Probably it's something really weird about you.

So you start a new cluster.

Now maybe you get new-agey or alternative or "witchy".

And you do that cluster.

And on and on and on it goes, all the while you are being brought in closer to Her and you don't even know where you are heading. Your understanding of Her changes and morphs and is framed as a "phase", etc. only to be brought around to face Her in a new way. She may be a male deity. She may be Nature Spirits. She may be Animism or a Death

Goddess. She may be an ancient culture or living on the land or your sudden fascination with mythology.

Round and round you will go. And that Call will be the start of it. And each time you think you are finally there, please remember, on this path, there is no "there". It's okay though, you will believe, absolutely believe, you finally got there - that what you are interested in, that what you understand, is IT. And that IT is an essential part of the path - it's the nature of The Pull.

Seventeen

THE PULL

The Pull is a funny one. Remember the first diagram in The Three-fold nature of Initiation: Overview section? The one that shows The Call, The Pull, and The Metamorphosis? At the bottom of that first diagram was this:

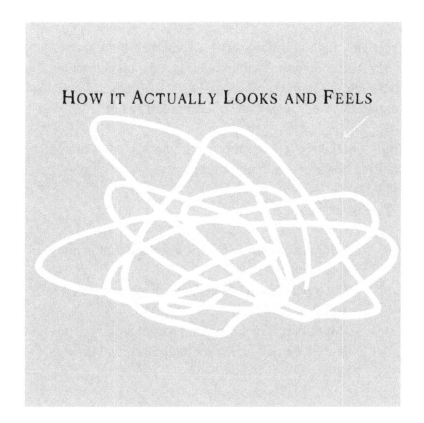

How it Actually Looks and Feels

The Pull is often a sudden, necessary interest in something. It's often something you view as essential following the revelation of The Call. The Pull is what gets you to dive in. And it's the way you dive in.

The Pull will occupy your whole field of vision and seem like you MUST study/do/learn/become whatever The Pull is indicating. It can seem like a complete pivot out of whatever your current life is, like a career change or a return to school or becoming a poet or the need to purchase 10 books on a topic or converting your dining room into an art space because you are going to be the best paper flower artist of all time.

You will think you have ADD. Or you will think this is just your ADD. I personally think ADD is a fantastic feature She puts into so many of us. It makes the process of Initiation, especially the Pull phase, sooooo much easier.

But the Pull isn't just about pursuing a new interest or getting obsessed with something.

The Pull serves several functions:

> 1) It gets you away from something that is not serving you
> 2) It awakens and feeds something necessary or useful
> 3) It gets you to a place, a time, or a person you need to experience something essential for your path

We cannot see, or even fathom, the great web of existence and our place in it. We cannot see the places the threads that we walk will lead us. We cannot know, from places of true wisdom, what best steps to take or choices to make. We can know that some choices are better than others. We can suss-out themes in our paths. But the greater field of being in which we belong is too vast and too complex and too ancient for even the brightest and wisest of us to know.

If we can understand this, if we can be humble enough to accept this, then we can begin to walk this path well. We can also begin to see how mind-blowing is the wisdom, and dare I say love, inherent in the initiatory path.

We are, all of us, essentially flying blind in life, even when we know we are on a path and are clear about our "purpose". The Pull of the initiatory path gets us to go to the places we need to be and discover what we need to discover and cultivate what we need to cultivate in ourselves to further our initiatory journey. Most of the time we don't even know it's happening. And even less do we understand the profundity of the twists and turns.

Have you ever had an experience that was devastating or horrific only to feel later that you understand why it needed to happen? Usually it's after you meet someone who is in a dark or needful place, a crisis, and you happen to be the only person for miles around who could actually help them in the way they truly need?

Or have you ever been obsessed with learning something, thinking it's your calling or path in life, only to leave it and move on to something else. Then, often years later, find your real love and realize that the thing you learned, often the seemingly many "useless" things you have learned, all are relevant or useful in some way to your new, deeper way of living?

On my own path, the many learnings I have collected invariably become relevant with someone I'm working with. It may be an obscure interest they have that I happen to have immersed myself in once upon a time that makes them feel more welcomed or understood with me. It may be some nutrition tidbit I picked up or a chunk of knowledge about a point in history or an ancient culture. It may be a gnarly experience I have been through. There always seems to be a use for the things I have collected along the path of being Pulled.

Sometimes The Pull isn't about getting you information or skills, but about putting you in the right exact time in history you need to be in. And sometimes it's about getting your path and another person's path to collide so you can meet.

What is important to understand about The Pull is that it is active and that it serves multiple purposes. Also that we might not understand what the purpose might be or that the things we encounter in the pull will be useful. Or that it may only be useful one time in the very different future but that it will matter. Sometimes we will never understand how it matters.

You can see how growing our capacity for the nature of The Pull actually serves us on the initiatory path. The jerking around, the confusion, the frustration, the seemingly being all over the place, which are all qualities of The Pull, help us cultivate the temperament for the path.

What you need to walk the path, the path itself will give or lead you to, eventually.

The more you observe this, the more you see how this phenomenon has been working in your own life (evidence journal this please!) the more obvious the Intelligence that permeates all things actually is. This helps ease our anxieties and uncertainties and control tendencies. Which all make the next phase of the initiatory path, metamorphosis, easier to bear.

Eighteen

METAMORPHOSIS

The first thing I want to say about metamorphosis is that the essence of what is happening in the Initiatory process is that we are being brought into alignment with the greater field of being. In this particular process with the Great Mother, we are being brought into alignment with Her, to be both emissaries and vessels.

This may help as you go through metamorphosis, to understand you are being made *into* something. You aren't transforming for no purpose or randomly.

Metamorphosis itself is the hardest part of initiation. In The Call and The Pull we encounter the need for change that is, until it has actually happened, theoretical. We are in a process. Metamorphosis is when we have actually undergone genuine change. This means we cannot go back to what we were. Roads close. Certain opportunities that we once could have taken had we wanted to, are no longer possible. Certain relationships simply cannot continue.

There is a closing off of pathways that have provided us with security, or the possibility of security should we need it. And because we have not yet been in the world as this new version, this changed self, we have to learn new rules and ways to navigate that we do not initially have.

Metamorphosis, then, is like leaping off a dark cliff at night - you have no idea how far down it is or what you are leaping into - swords? Monsters? A soft enormous pillow? It's genuinely terrifying.

Even if I tell you exactly what you are becoming, even if I write an entire book on it, even if you are given orientation and tools and comfort, *the lived experience of something is fundamental to our understanding and our comfort.* No amount of thoughts or words or information can replace that.

The entire process of initiation is disorienting. But the actual transformation, or, more specifically, the moment just before the actual transformation where the transformation is inevitable and necessary, is the most terrifying.

Most people think they have to be willing to lose everything - their jobs, their marriages, their friends and families. They think they will have to forfeit material comforts. I imagined, in my early initiation cycles, that this certainly would be the case, and it tormented me.

The Call and the Pull both alert us to the fact that we can no longer live or be a certain way in the world. Because that is all we have known, and because we have no idea what transformation is like, and because our modern world is not exactly the ecosystemic, interrelated healthy example of community it should be, we may have trust issues that if we fall, no one will catch us. Because very often our experience is that we are truly the only one holding us up.

So not knowing what you are becoming, and not knowing, experientially, in a lived way, what this thing you are becoming will be like in the world, you don't know if you will be able to hold yourself up. This can be panic-inducing. It is, in a very real way, terrifying.

The majority of people who come to me during their initiatory experiences come with the most desperation and fear during the Metamorphosis stage. Everything up to this point still feels kind of optional compared to this. Metamorphosis is irreversible.

This is why I talk so much about the need to break the habit of hyper-independence. And why I keep saying that we need to become more relational. The hyper-independent mind, the habituation to isolation, the inability to function interdependently, make the process of metamorphosis excruciating.

Learning to be more relational and interdependent, like simply learning healthy communication and sharing one's needs and asking for help, all soften the impact of the very real vulnerability of change.

When you are in the throes on initiation, you are likely going to reach out for help. Whether or not you are able to find the strange help that you need depends on a number of things. But I will tell you that many folks you find will likely view you through the lens of pathology. After all, you might seem manic, psychotic, or otherwise unstable. Indeed, you may *be* these things for a bit here and there. That is part of breaking away from the Field of Denial. It's part of breaking away from a self that is conditioned to very different things than one who is walking this path.

Having a sense of the initiatory process will give you some language. It will help you get oriented. It will help you communicate what is happening to you and perhaps open the possibility that you find someone who can be with you when it is most crucial.

One thing you can, and I would say should, do throughout this process is to communicate with Them of the Unseen. Start an altar practice. Learn how to give offerings and otherwise be in right-relationship with the Unseen Beings of this world. In part six of this book I offer info about this. You should be cultivating some of these things before you are desperate. It will be a lovely investment to make in yourself. If you are already desperate, start some of these practices before you do anything else.

There are no guarantees on this path. There is no "do this and you will for sure have that outcome". This forces us to be humble. It forces us into desperation. For humility and desperation are two things that will crack us open enough for Her to be able to truly come in.

Part Five:

Three Phases of the Initiatory Path

Nineteen

THE FOUR PATHS OVERVIEW

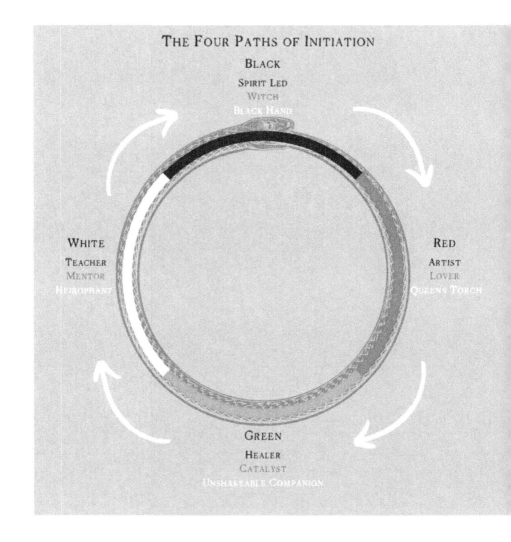

THE FOUR PATHS OF INITIATION

BLACK
SPIRIT LED
WITCH
BLACK HAND

WHITE
TEACHER
MENTOR
HEIROPHANT

RED
ARTIST
LOVER
QUEENS TORCH

GREEN
HEALER
CATALYST
UNSHAKEABLE COMPANION

The Four Paths of Initiation are Black, Red, Green, and White. In the chapters that follow, we will be going over each of these in detail. For now, I want to walk you through an overview of how this works so that you can begin to play with your understanding and how this applies to your own initiatory experience.

The first thing to know is that you will cultivate the qualities of each of the four paths at various points in your initiatory journey. The point is not to decide which of the paths you are primarily walking, but to be open to what reveals itself to you as you gain understanding of each of these paths. It may be that one of the paths is the main focus of your life, or it may be that you gain tremendous proficiency in two or more. It may also be that a deep dive into one path creates the proficiencies and generates the experiences you need to get to another path you are meant to be on, making it so the path you thought you were meant for was merely a stepping stone.

All paths lead us to a deeper relationship with Her.

Knowledge of the Four Paths will not only give you insight and understanding, it may help reveal what has been invisible or not-yet-validated for you. So as you read the chapters on each of the Four Paths, you will find resonance and ah-ha's that will fill in much for you.

All of us born to the Dragon Mother come in through the Black Path. We come in deeply connected with the beings of the Unseen Realm. They teach and guide us in our early years. Dream allies, nature spirits, and familiars might all reveal themselves as "invisible friends" or we may simply have a sense of friendship and care with animals and wind and the many other beings around us.

Those of us born on the Black Path come in *strange*. Whether this is a physical or neurological abnormality, a strong personality, or noticeable gifts, whether intellectual, creative, or of the Red, Green, or White path. There may be a strange connection with animals or unusual interests or we may say and do odd things. Black Path children may also just seem "off", even labeled disabled in some way, be seen as difficult, "touched", or in some other way, unusual.

Each of us tends to develop along the lines of the Paths as outlined here, though the green path might come before red, as it did with me and many others.

We are born to the Black Path then, as children, tend to begin to play along the Red Path either with dancing or art or writing or performance or singing or music. Next, the Green Path shows up when the child begins to show concern for other beings and attempts various forms of healing care or of ministering to those beings around them. They will be very concerned with the welfare of others, either generally or a particular kind of being - other children, dogs, insects, and the like. The White Path first shows up as the urge to teach others things. In children this can look like wanting to share knowledge, an intense focus on learning - usually one specific arena, or playing "teacher", "priest", or even "parent".

If you have spent much time around children, you may be thinking that all children exhibit these characteristics to varying degrees. While this may be true, those of us born to

Her will tend to be taken up with one of these paths to a more intense degree or with more of a "gift" or voraciousness than other children. We will do things that are unusual. We may seem more mature, like a child of the Red Path may seem "inappropriately" sensual or "advanced" for their age, whether this be physically or artistically. A child of the Green Path will study some form of healing, or many forms, and feel the need to tend to those around them, being the "helper" to those even to their own detriment.

While many children may exhibit various characteristics in these paths, those of us born to Her tend to not leave these paths. In other words, we don't "move on". One of these paths begins to get more attention and we gain more proficiency in it. The child who likes to draw or sing is suddenly "very, very good" without receiving instruction. Or, the child wants to immerse themselves in the things of their path more than they want to do other things. So their spare time is devoted to cultivating their interests on this path. Or they use the things of their path to regulate themselves. It can be quite difficult to dissuade them from their interests.

You will notice in the diagram that there are arrows that suggest going around and around. As I said, each of us will tend to develop proficiency of some kind in each of these four areas. Where we focus is the area that gets the most development and the area that we then progress through.

We can make hundreds of rounds, spending more or less time in one area or another, in a lifetime. Just in childhood, you will go through a number of rounds just by the time you reach your teens.

As you move through your initiatory journey, you will find yourself pulled into one of the Four Paths at various points. Remember when we talked about The Call, The Pull, and Metamorphosis? And remember how that journey might look like you are going all over the place and it seems to make no sense? And remember we talked about themes to your clusters of change?

Well, if you combine that understanding with the information presented here about the Four Paths, you may recognize that your Call, Pull, and Metamorphosis processes have dragged you through gaining basic proficiencies in each of these Four Paths.

Whatever Path or Paths you have not yet developed a basic proficiency in, know it is coming at some point. For example, though we are all born to the Black path, yet many of us do not connect to the Unseen Realm until much later in our journey, after we have exhausted nearly every other available method. This is largely due to the taboo nature of the Black Path.

In the diagram you will see the title of the path, i.e. "Green", then you will see the basic level of the expression of that path, i.e. "Healer". The next iteration is in lighter print below it. In this case that would be "Facilitator" and then the lightest is "Unshakeable Companion". This structure reveals increasingly advanced degrees of development and commitment and wisdom of each of the Four Paths. It also reveals how we transform into Her hands and hearts in this world. In other words, the final stage of any particular path shows the kind of vessel we become for Her and the function this serves in the world.

Every one of these paths results in others having an experience of Her in some way through us. We are transformed so much that others will actually feel Her presence through us much more than they will feel us. This is because, after sufficient initiation, there isn't much of the individual left - our presence becomes a way for others to have a more direct experience of Her according to their Wyrd and according to what She sees that they need or that She wants from them. We become a part of the greater ecosystem of Her.

For those of us that move into the Ocean of Initiation, the Four Paths become essentially irrelevant as we all then work to become Hers so completely that our function and path give way to much stranger and deeper things. We go off the map and into the Primal. We are less vessels for her and more Her *as* us.

Those of us that are fated to transformation into the lightest print in one of the Four Paths, i.e. Black Hand, Queen's Torch, Unshakeable Companion, Hierophant, tend to have this theme as our occupation in some way. Or it permeates the rest of our lives to a degree that there is no hiding what we are.

Of the Four Paths, the two that are most taboo or maligned are certainly the Black and the Red. And the two that are most "acceptable", and exploited, are the Green and the White. All of these paths can be "performed" by people linked with the Field of Denial to exploit and gain power. All of these paths can be done well or poorly. Until we are truly rooted in the Great Mother and the greater ecosystem of belonging, we are at risk of being led astray or becoming exploitative or performative.

Please note: in modern society, where we have lost rooting in the deeper way of things, few of us have encounters with real power. This means that for someone who gains a tiny bit of power, they may believe they are quite powerful and advanced. Because, in a comparative context, they are. But in the context of Her and those who truly serve Her, they would be like flies in a tornado. This is something to keep in mind. You may believe yourself to be powerful, but do not let it go to your head. For no matter how much power you may gain in this life, you, and I, are always only ants and always only what we are according to Her favor.

Therefore, let us, before we worry too much about how powerful we are, or not, at least traverse the Paradox of Existence thoroughly, so we can hold the truth of both how we might be favored and of our own nothingness. Then we can engage such topics if we still need to according to some tiny measure of wisdom.

What you will learn as you go round and round the cycle of the initiatory paths is that there is one common theme to each. Every single initiatory path the Dragon Mother pulls you down requires advocacy: advocacy on behalf of innocence, advocacy for the self, advocacy on behalf of the reality that exists beyond, and in spite of, the human-created.

She will require you speak out from the deep heart of belonging, on behalf of the right to exist as the holy moments that all beings are. Morality will be your shield, absence of morality your sword. For true advocacy is not on human terms, but Hers.

Let's take a closer look at each of the Four Paths.

Twenty

THE BLACK PATH

Spirit-led, Witch, Black Hand

Of the four paths, the most maligned and the most misunderstood is the Black Path. The Black path is, very simply, all about relationship with the Unseen realm.

In modern times, especially given the predominance of Christian influence in the western world, the Unseen has been slathered with connotations of evil. Even for non-Christians who have grown-up in western culture, the fear that you are being "deceived by demons" can arise when you consciously encounter your first spirit(s), or merely consider this path.

We all come in through the Black Path. In other words, we all come from the realm of spirit into bodies to be in this, the Seen, realm. As such, we all have ties to the Unseen and the beings therein.

When we are born here, these ties give us a profound connection to the very alive world around us. We tend to have a felt sense of family with the entirety of the world in which we live. But it also means that the spirit(s) that are bound to us guide and inform and protect us - whether a dead grandma or a familiar spirit or something else.

For me, I have always had dreams of spirits teaching me things. And I also had a profound relationship with the natural world. I was constantly being protected and aided and I was constantly being "instructed" on how to listen to, and interact with, the wild world around me.

This was all completely "normal" to me, the same way it is completely normal to every strange-souled child ever born. So normal that we don't usually notice it as different from anything else. At least, not until we get older and go "Oh, I guess it wasn't like that for everyone".

Many children lose their innate connection to the Unseen around the age of 6. This is about the time outer-world indoctrination and influence begin to take over.

So the Black Path often fades into the background.

Until, as teenagers, we discover "weird shit" like ouija boards and tarot cards and clove cigarettes.

Depending on your Wyrd and depending on your path, you may or may not reawaken to the Black Path to intentionally walk it and deepen in it. But you are always on it because you are born to it.

However else your path unfolds, and whatever path you may believe to be yours, please know that with initiations of the Dragon Mother, you are ALWAYS spirit-led. As such, it behooves you, even if you do not choose to actively work with spirits like a witch might, to give offerings to land spirits, ancestors, and your familiar(s). At the very least, you should always give offerings to the Great Being that is the Beginning of All Things - the one we might call Dragon Mother.

It is the fact that we are spirit-led that we feel The Call, The Pull, and go through Metamorphosis. It is the fact that we are spirit-led that any other path we walk is even possible. The Spirits are always with us and always a factor in our lives.

The Black Path is the foundation upon which all other paths rest. If you want to gain proficiency in any of these paths, you are absolutely dependent on your relationship with the Unseen. Not only do They teach, guide, and protect, but they potentize and synchronize.

If you want to be a great healer, you must have good relationships with the Unseen - whether plant spirits, Healers like Mengloth or Ninti, the land spirits where you are, ancestors, or any number of ways you may be pulled. In other words, you need proficiency in the Black Path to deepen your abilities as a Healer.

The spirits help us in more ways than most can imagine. The Black Path should be the ground you stand upon as you engage any other pursuits. The Great Red Serpent Herself requires this as our ground. You cannot work with Her, belong to Her, and serve Her if you do not know how to talk with Her, propitiate Her, and give thanks to Her.

Making the Black path the core to anything else you do - learning how to be in right-relationship, study, ritual, offerings, journeying - will greatly aid you on your path.

At some point, whether the Black Path is your primary path or not, you will be required to become witched.

Becoming witched is part of the metamorphosis of this initiatory journey. As we go around and around, we deepen. As we deepen, we encounter territory where we need aid and strange help. The more aid and strange help we need, the more strange we must become to receive the attention of these beings. We must become something else, something more.

You *will* come to a point in your initiatory journey where you are required to leave what you have known. You *will* reach a point in your path where you need help that is beyond the purview of human knowledge. You *will* encounter territory where your client or lover or student or family member is in crisis that the law and medicine and any other human avenue is impotent to help. Perhaps you are the one who gets beyond the reach of what the human realm can do for you in your moment of greatest crisis. The realm we turn to is the Unseen. The beings we turn to are *strange*.

How much more likely are They to aid us, to meet what we ask for, if we, ourselves, have shown we are worthy of Their aid? Because we show respect. Because we know how to offer. Because we give offerings. Because we have spoken with them and made ourselves known to Them countless times - at rivers, at crossroads, at our altar, in circle, in the black of night, when we ask, and gain permission, before we take from nature, and the many other ways They have come to look kindly upon us?

Walking the path of the Dragon Mother means going

outside the human-created and seeking the friendship and guidance and protection and aid and favor of Them of the Unseen. Because this path *requires it*.

And so you become a Witch. Call it Sorcerer if you prefer. Call it Priestess if you prefer.

These days it is very popular to "be a witch". So I am going to define for you what I mean by this for the purposes of this book.

There are, essentially, two types of witch:

There is the witch who exerts her will onto the world around her to achieve her desired outcomes (witch can be any gender). This witch must raise power to power her spells and workings, which can leave her exhausted. It's a good reason to work with a coven, so that many people can raise the power needed to power spells and workings. This type of witch very often has "power over" spirits and tends to think in terms of commanding them to do their bidding. This type of witch also feels comfortable calling on beings they have no relationship with in various kinds of workings - like a love spell and calling on Aphrodite when they have never made an offering to Aphrodite in their life. This kind of witch is not predominantly spirit-relational, or of the Black Path.

The other kind of witch *is* spirit-relational. Their spells and workings are done in partnership with the greater ecology of beings. Their workings are powered by beings far more ancient and powerful than they. Their witch art is rooted in right-relationship and the greater ecosystem.

Because few people are conscious of this delineation, there are many witches who say they love and respect nature and unseen spirits yet never engage in right-relationship and spend their time ordering these beings around without noticing the conflict there.

This is not an intentional admonishment to anyone. And it's not black/white territory. I am bringing this up so you can really think about what you are doing and how you are doing and why you are doing. I do not personally believe it wise to use your own energy to power workings. Nor do I believe it wise to boss around spirits or to work with spirits you have no real relationship with.

On the Black Path, becoming a witch is becoming one who actively works with spirits as an essential part of your lived reality. It means making a pact where you get the green light from a greater Spirit, like the Master of Spirits or the Great Mother, Hekate or Cernunnos, the Great Horned One or Freya, to be bound in relationship with them *so that* you can become truly strange-souled.

Becoming truly strange-souled, or witch-souled, means making a commitment to the Black Path and to being in right-relationship in the greater ecology of beings. You see and experience the Greater Intelligence in all things. As such, you tend to respect Life. It also means you release the iron-grip on concepts of human morality and live more naturally - where predator and prey are not demeaned but honored. Where you do and act on behalf of the ecosystem and your sacred place in it. Where you learn the nature of the Spirit Realm and the nature of the Beings there and how they interact in our world and how to interact with them, either in visions, dreams, or waking life.

Being a Witch means you are a part of the greater web and you do not "command" but you participate. You understand the Great Hunt might take one from your own home so you do things that might get them to pass you and yours by. Or whatever your traditions and ancient wisdoms reveal about how to be in relationship with Them.

You can be a witch however you want. But if you are on an initiatory path of the Dragon Mother, it is absolutely relational. At some point it will be required, so best to start now if you haven't already.

The deeper you go as a Witch-souled person walking the Black Path, the stranger things become. You will believe and act in ways that are increasingly conventionally taboo. You will learn that the preferred offerings of certain beings is your own blood, perhaps mixed with some cream or whiskey. You will give attention to spirits others might view as "demonic'. You will function much more in the gray areas, not taking moral stands so much as ecosystemic ones. You will insist on community over the individual. You will feel a growing sense of belonging and obligation to the whole.

Your sense of the sacredness of life will increase and you will tend to treat other beings much better. Your acceptance of hardship and death will also increase and you will treat these experiences differently than others, which may disturb them.

Many witches are about how much power they can

accumulate for themselves. Black Path witches are about how much they can transform to be vessels for the Deeper Powers to come into this world through them. You certainly gain true power this way, but you want this power for Them and for the community of beings in which you belong, it's never just for yourself. Though it is certainly appropriate, and I might say even necessary, to ask for things for the safety and well-being of you and yours.

Any truly good Healer on this path is a witch. Any truly good Teacher on this path is a Witch. Any truly good Artist on this path is a Witch.

Because becoming witch-souled is the only way you can gain the insights and abilities you need to truly master the art you practice - whether it is Lover, Healer, Witch, or Teacher. And to master your path, you absolutely need the insight and wisdom and power only They can give.

Becoming a Black Hand is the last, what we might call, most extreme stage of the Black Path.

You will notice the last stage of each path is where the greatest transformation is seen.

Becoming a Black Hand means you act and do and think and feel increasingly in alignment with the greater ecosystem of reality. This is true of every one of these Paths. It just happens to have the flavor of the Black Path. Perhaps you write books on sorcery? Perhaps you start a school or society for other spirit-led folk? Perhaps you create a temple to Hekate?

All paths in their most realized expression serve to bring more and more people ever closer to Her. The Black Hand does this in their own spooky way.

The Black Hand is a very strange person indeed. As Black Hand, your spirit-art will be in depths few will ever achieve or dare go. You will likely be feared except by other strange-souled folks and possibly animals or children. The Black Hand is where the adept truly becomes a vessel to the Deeper Powers as few of us will ever know Them.

Twenty-one

THE RED PATH

Artist, Lover, Queen's Torch

The Red Path is the other path that is maligned and misunderstood. It is characterized by exuberance, expression, and what we might call "excess". Red Path people seem to have life just spilling out of them with a need to give it form.

The Artist on the Red Path may be a dancer, a writer, a painter, a musician, a poet, an actor, or any other person giving creative expression to the force of Her that is within and around them. They have life flowing into and through them and they must circulate it, often via their creative medium or through direct sharing.

Red Path people also tend to be very sensual. This may or may not be sexual. They tend to be touch, smell, taste, sight, and/or sound aroused. They are inspired by life around and in them. They feel joy in existing - often quite unselfconsciously.

Red Path people very often go from Artist to Lover when they realize others do not feel the joy or love of this world the way they do and they can see the toll this takes on them. Even if this is not conscious, Red Path people are compelled to bring life to places. In the Red Path, the Dragon Mother might guide them to people who need a kind of enlivening that only the intimacy that the Lover can reach.

When the Red Path person shifts from Artist to Lover, we often see the emergence of the Sacred Prostitute. This can take many forms. But it is characterized by sexual intimacy, often including relational intimacy, where the Lover is drawn to a person, not for their own interests, but for how their ability to love might benefit another.

The way this works, whether or not one pursues actual sex work, is that the Red Path person is attracted, or compelled, to be with someone who needs healing or life awakened in them, like they need to be reminded of the sacred. Or they need to have an experience of the sacred through the body of, and experience with, the Lover.

The Lover embodies the sacred in a way that allows someone else to experience it who, on their own, would otherwise be unable. And they *need* this experience. They do not seek, or cannot find, healing in other ways. Or they cannot allow it. So the Lover comes. We can also say: the Lover goes where she is sent.

Often, when the experience with the Lover is complete, whether in an evening or a matter of years, the person who benefitted from the Lover "moves on", better for the experience. They often then find their life partner or get a promotion or have some other boon come to them after they have been filled with the life force the Lover brings.

The Lover is often left depleted or worse off or somehow delayed or set-back or simply just invisible. Theirs is not a path of achievement, but of exposing people to Her sacred flame - of reminding people of the sacred moment and the preciousness of this life and flowing it into another's body and being.

The Red Path person is often dominated by innocence. This innocence allows them to be used by Her without becoming jaded or harmed by their immersion in the dark and fractured places of others, which is precisely what enables them to penetrate deadness and distortions.

Innocence is the sacred buffer.

As the Red Path person matures, as they see their pattern of being used in this way, as they come to need and want more for themselves because being the Lover eventually exhausts them, they are invited or pulled into becoming the Queen's Flame.

The Queen's Flame lights the way for those lost in the dark. She (or he or they) begins to understand the role they have played and becomes a more active participant in their own path. This is the point where the Lover matures around their own innocence and understands that, while leading with innocence is beautiful for what it is, there is something more.

That more is where the Lover must claim the power and knowledge they carry by putting Innocence into the background. They must work through the shame of their own aliveness. What a strange thing to say, isn't it? But the

FOD shames those who are truly alive. The FOD say you are "too much" - too sexual, too sensual, too sensitive, too open, too loose, too weird, too wild, too creative, too unstructured.

The Artist allows Life to come through them. The Lover brings that life to others who are in need of it. The Queen's Torch stands rooted in her truth - unashamed of her sensual, alive nature, rooted in the wisdom of it and the world's need of it. She begins to see how parched and empty and shriveled people are, even as they might "have it all", she sees from a distance, understanding that their fire is their own to tend.

The Queen's Torch stands in Her light, unashamed, ready to show others the way to their own source of Life, which is available to all. The Queen's Torch does not compromise herself for others. She no longer sinks so that others may swim. She no longer gives away her magic and power to boost those who have closed themselves off to Life's succulence.

On the Red Path, the flow opens with the Artist. Then the Lover stretches us past convention by making us able to bring love to ugly places, places hidden by the one the Lover blesses, places marked as taboo or unloveable by both society and the very person the Lover brings her sacred innocence to. The Lover grows an ability to see and exist in places Love might otherwise never be able to penetrate. This cultivated ability, over time, grows power in the Lover so that they might become the Queen's Torch.

By claiming the strength that this kind of loving of others

requires, the shame and taboo fall away from the Lover, stripping her of a layer of FOD, so that she may step into this world as the Queen's Torch, majestic, and ready and able to love those who are unlovable and in need of being led to the Great Mother in a more direct, open, and even demanding way. There is no more going into the secret darkness of others. The Queen's Torch brings light to all, and is a warm flame that invites people closer to the Great Mother.

Those who encounter people on the Red Path will feel an intimate acceptance that perhaps not even the Healer can achieve. They, perhaps more than any other, can sit in the shit of humanity and allow the transformative power of their innocent love to awaken the beauty in the ugliest of places.

You can see how essential the Red Path is to the Green and the White and the Black, can't you? You can see how the ability to not be repulsed by whatever one may find in another will so greatly serve Her, don't you? How profound the gifts of sensuality and innocence of the Red Path, for it allows us to allow more of Her to reach more people more potently through us.

May we be humbled by the brilliance of Her ways. And may we be able, with the true heart of the Red Path, love what is unloveable.

Twenty-two

THE GREEN PATH

Healer, Catalyst, Unshakeable Companion

The Green Path is the path of the Healer. Its iterations: Healer, Catalyst, and Unshakeable Companion, are all expressions of the Healer as the Healer gains experience and maturity.

Being an Initiatory Path, the stages of the Green Path serve as their own initiations.

The Healer may start off as a child or an adult. The Green Path arose in me at the age of two and was the first path that grabbed and held me and led me to the other doorways that each of the paths are.

The Healer has an urge to help in a way that alleviates some kind of pain. Their response to suffering is one of compassion and care with an urge to ameliorate the suffering. The Healer wants to make people healthy again.

The path of the Healer requires us to navigate so much of what it means to be, not only human, but to be alive. Healers often face death and illness, trauma and pain, vulnerability and fear. We sit with people in some of the most difficult or tender places of their lives, usually behind closed doors. We aid and comfort and occasionally cure.

Many people think of a healer as "person who cures". The beginning for many Healers is an intent to cure or eliminate that which causes suffering. But as we increasingly immerse ourselves in the wounded and hurting places of other humans, so much more occurs.

We get exposed to things like lack of means someone might be dealing with that obstructs the healing they need, which forces us to confront socioeconomic disparity. We experience abusive relationships behind adrenal fatigue and immune disorders, making us confront systems of power and abuse. We experience human systems that are not designed to care for people, but to milk them dry and dispose of them. We are faced with the frustration of how temporary the relief we bring may be. We are also faced with not being able to bring relief.

Healers are allowed into places in people's lives even their closest family may not be allowed.

The Healer, on the initiatory path, is constantly going to be exposed to their own limitations - of skill, of knowledge, of capacity, and of compassion. The Healer will be confronted with where their own patterns of the FOD limit or harm their clients. The Healer will need to deal with the ways they are impacted by their clients and the gaping maw of need that exists in the world and how they might be being made ill or overly tired or drained to the point that they are no longer effective as a Healer.

The burn-out that Healers face, along with all the other things listed here, are part of what pulls a Healer into the path of the Catalyst.

At some point the Healer realizes their limits, and the limit of trying to do the heavy lifting for people. Even Healers who educate and offer classes and programs and courses, are often lugging people around because the FOD steeps us all in parent/child hierarchies, even as adults.

What I mean by this is that the Field of Denial exists in a delusion of hierarchy that places someone at the top in such a way as they are in a parental role. This means those below them are often infantilized or treated as children - they are yelled at or ignored or patronized or made less-than. This means that clients often unconsciously put themselves in the position of helplessness or ignorance or lack of personal accountability for their experiences and put the healer in the position of being responsible for them, often as they might have wishes a parent would have been, or they make the healer the "expert" in a way that is unhealthy, enmeshed, or codependent.

At some point, the Healer begins to see through the limitations and the antagonists within the models and beliefs and methods they use, and that permeate the Field of Denial. They begin to get more real with their clients and shift from "helping" to simply holding space that is powerfully honest and human and safe. This also means they reach outside of their training and begin to look at larger, more culturally diverse human systems.

The more a Healer does this, the more they begin to see

changes, often subtle, to the way clients respond. They begin to hear from clients that just being in their presence helps. They begin to see that they need less severe or drastic or expensive methods to get the same, or better, outcomes. They begin to experience more "miracles" with clients.

This is when the Healer becomes the Catalyst.

The Catalyst is the Healer who has grown so much capacity and is steeped in so much experience and humility that they see through pain and illness, or see pain and illness in a radically new light. They see the human being. The meaning of illness and pain changes. The Catalyst does not feel an urgent need to erase people's suffering. Their priority shifts from "curing" to deepening. Their priority shifts from "helping" to holding. Their priority shifts from "doing" to engaging and activating.

By the time the Healer becomes the Catalyst, clients are usually getting way more from engagement with them than ever before or with other healers. The Catalyst will hear things like "I got more from one session with you than seven years of therapy" coupled with a genuine rooting of the client in a commitment to lived changed and personal accountability for their own well-being. When I say "personal accountability", please understand this includes that our clients begin to come out of the delusion of hyper-independence and isolation and accepts that relationships can, and do, affect their health and they begin to learn to be more relationally skillful.

The Catalyst often is called into people's lives when no

cure is possible but healing is needed in the form of permission or acceptance. Where the Healer never gives up, the Catalyst gives permission for *what is.*

By the time we have truly become the Catalyst, our presence is reassuring, potent, and creates ease in people just by connection with us.

Catalysts also tend to activate people's shit as well as their wellness. Catalysts stir people up just by existing. Catalysts dwell beyond the scope of healing. Their presence brings a kind of pure gaze, free of judgment and intolerance, that offers clarity and movement to those who are ready for it. This pure gaze is one many are pained to be seen by.

When the Healer becomes Catalyst, a new awareness and sense of responsibility must accompany the shift.

The Catalyst must understand the effect that their presence has on others so that they can be responsible in their discernment of who they will and won't work with. Where a Healer may take on people in their chosen field - physical or psychological - the Catalyst only takes on people who are in a place of readiness and have an ability or a desperate need for who and what they are.

The Healer can help anyone they are trained to help without much fall-out. The worst that will happen is that they are unable to help or that they waste a client's time and money.

The Catalyst can actually cause immense disruption in

those who are not ready for deeper levels of healing and change. This is because the Catalyst catalyzes people into deeper honesty and presence within themselves and the world. The Catalysts, intentionally or not, brings to the surface things that are hidden. This is not the purview of the Healer - not in the way and to the degree that happens with a Catalyst.

Unfortunately, many Healers who have catalyst experiences get a little power trippy and enjoy the breakdowns they cause or the triggers they activate in others, taking it to be a sign of their power. This is not kind. It is often self-serving and cruel and is the basis for much of the manipulation and toxicity that passes as helping in our modern world. Making people uncomfortable by what you "see" is easy. Being a person where a person can be seen in a way that creates a genuine possibility for transformation is only possible when we are not trying to stimulate their defenses or push their buttons, no matter how "helpful" or "potent" we may think it is.

The genuine experience of activating people (as opposed to the power trip of it) develops the Catalyst in ways that prepare them for being an Unshakeable Companion.

The Unshakeable Companion is an expert in existing as a human in this world. They have faced the darkest, most horrible situations. They have grown past the horror and tension of what life does to us and what we do with life.

The Unshakeable Companion has been through their own shredding and has grown their capacity for anything life throws at the person who needs them. They are immovable in their ability to sit with any pain. They can bring comfort to terror, fearlessness to rage, soothing to existential crisis, laughter to suffering, and grounding to the most torrential disorientation.

The Unshakeable Companion roots into the Mother's truth. They have seen into the Primal and know it is horror and chaos, beauty and joy. They do not need to fixate on a moment because they know all moments have a beginning, a middle, and an end. They are not attached to what the end may be or how the moment itself is playing out. Any particular moment doesn't mean anything more than the need for our presence that the person experiencing it has.

Understand that by the time a healer has become an Unshakeable Companion, their expertise, ease, and skill come easily and permeate their interactions. They often are able to nearly immediately see underlying patterns and infuse their presence with useful tools. However, the Unshakeable Companion will often also see the wisdom or need for a human to have the experience they are having, that deeper wisdom is in the experience, and will thus know where to lean in to help and where to allow. This can feel profoundly cruel to clients who cannot access this wisdom.

The Unshakeable Companion feels both acceptance and sadness or joy for whatever experience they are a part of. There is no need to choose or label. This is terrible and it *is*. This is beautiful and it *is*. None of it means anything and it means everything and we sit with it without needing to run.

Where the Healer may be involved for many months or years with their clients, the Catalyst is usually in it for a few months or even just one encounter, and is often sought when a client needs their unique aid to shift into deeper alignment with themselves or their life in some way.

The Unshakeable Companion is often there for moments of greatest crisis and transition - leaving a domestic abuse situation, death, a terminal cancer diagnosis, to unshakeably witness the telling of childhood torture and simply hold the immensity of what this has done to a person and the fact that it is etched, irremoveable, into their soul. Or, quite often, as someone is in the throes of initiation themselves and they need the undistorted presence that only an Unshakeable Companion can offer in this place.

The Green Path grows our ability to see and face and hold and deal with what Life truly is. The Green Path rips away our preferences and aversions and moral stances and religious beliefs by demanding we be present with other beings with a purity and love and intimacy and distance few will ever understand.

The Green Path has great potential to kill us. Many of us get quite sick on this path. Because we are immersed in the sickness of humanity and because we grow to understand that what each person goes through is actually an experience they are having *because* of the community of humans in the world in which they live. This flies in the face of modern notions of "creating your own reality" and "pulling yourself up by your bootstraps" and "you can create anything if you work hard enough".

On the Green Path, we wake to the indisputable reality of interconnection. We get an intimate view into the impact that ecosystemic health and illness have on any one person. We come to see the essential, non-negotiable nature of need and of belonging. And we become living, breathing experiences of Her love and care that, when encountered by others, changes them in ways no conventional medicine or program or belief or experience can.

Those on the Green Path grow to bring the immensity of Her truth into embodied presence to be experienced undeniably, often incomprehensibly, by the people whose paths we cross. And these people are often forever changed, and we often never know the impact we've had, because we are always needed somewhere else.

Twenty-three

THE WHITE PATH

Teacher, Mentor, Hierophant

The White Path often begins once we have accumulated enough knowledge or skill to begin to pass to others. Though many on the White Path are those who simply love learning and assume others do, as well, they share what they are learning with anyone who will listen.

The path of Teacher is rich with initiatory learning. On this path, we come to see how imparting knowledge is insufficient. We come to see how people actually need to learn and we learn to modify our style and approach toward others' learning style so that they can actually benefit.

The White Path, like the Green, are both paths where there is an implicit permission to guide and help. Each path carries with it its own flavor of personal accountability, awareness of intent, and, at some point, the need to co-create relational space with others. The deeper any of us go into any of the paths, the more necessary, and required, relational integrity and awareness become.

As we learn to be a "good" Teacher, we are exposed to our own limits and also to the differences between "imparting" and "teaching". The Teacher is ever mindful of the student - their cues and signals, their openness and their resistance, and the degree to which they are engaged or glazed over. A good Teacher must cultivate their understanding of how people learn. This is not only about brain science, but also about things like motivation, unmet needs, life struggles, stress levels, hunger and sleep, and how relevant, or not, a person feels what the Teacher is teaching might be.

We must find the genuine motivation of the person we are teaching. We must create conditions that engender learning - trust, care, relevance, and support, and listening are all factors.

In the FOD teaching is often presented as if the teaching flows to the student, rather than the fact that both the teacher and the student are involved in learning. This is important to understand, especially given the reality that there are those who exploit this role to manipulate others to gain power, monetary wealth, and prestige.

If you are with a teacher who is not mindful of their responsibility as a teacher for your understanding, and who also makes learning, or lack of learning, solely your responsibility without creating ways to assist you, or sharing wisdom that will guide your learning path, be wary. There are many false gurus these days who exploit others and a hallmark is a lack of acknowledgement that both student and teacher are a part of the outcome.

A caution here, also, to students who want to hold a teacher accountable when they, themselves, are unwilling to do so with their own learning. As I said, the learning experience is shared. Some students are not right for some teachers, and vice versa. But both must engage from a place of personal accountability.

Once someone has been immersed in the White Path for some time, in other words, once a Teacher has matured, grown, mastered, and gained humility, they are often called to mentor.

The Mentor is someone who has a more comprehensive, internalized understanding of not only a subject or area of expertise, but they have been so cultivated by their time as a Teacher that they also have a great deal of insight and skillfulness with humans. They have not only grown their ability as teachers, but have also been sufficiently honed by their path as to have immense capacity as people themselves.

Being that the White Path *is* an initiatory path, we must understand one key element: we are not just learning to be good teachers, we are actually being used to transmit teachings. We are being used as mouthpieces of spiritual wisdom.

If you are on an initiatory path, you have undoubtedly experienced the phenomenon of something else taking over your communication, to the point where both your client/person you are interacting with and you go "whoa!". Where you wish you had a recording of what came out of your mouth because it was so right- on, wise, and profound. And so clearly not you speaking.

This phenomenon is one of the main outcomes of the

White Path, where we become dispensers of wisdom and guidance.

Many approach teaching like they are going to regurgitate what they've learned. On the White Path, you are actually getting "activated" by the need of another in a way that allows a transmission to come through for them.

On the White Path, we are increasingly cultivated as Her mouthpiece. We increasingly learn how to get out of the way of what comes through *instead of deciding what we teach.*

The Dragon Mother, indeed, any spirit being you work with, whether you know it or not, will put those on the initiatory path in the position to dispense wisdom and teachings.

These teachings are not human teachings.

The White Path is not where you teach what humans invented or created. The White Path is where you transmit the wisdom of the Great Mother to meet the need any one person has of Her in a moment.

What this feels, like, and this will be the same, or similar, to the other three paths, is that of being taken over and "poured through". The key with this is that we are activated by the need of another.

It's why, for anyone on the White Path, it is smart to design courses or workshops with a general outline of your topic but with plenty of room for Her to come in and do what She wants in that space. You can also ask your participants ahead of time what they are needing and wanting to create space for Her wisdom to come into the course materials you create, or the flow the course will take.

I have done workshops where I came in to talk about something and She took it over and it became an entirely different thing. This was a PAID workshop. People had paid to get the information and skill I was teaching. We started off, She came in, and it turned into an Oracle event, not a human one. Every single person there felt blessed and not a single person asked for their money back or complained it wasn't what they signed up for.

On the White Path, we would do well to incorporate wiggle room for these kinds of take-overs by Her.

This means you figure out a way to give people a heads-up about what kind of phenomenon may happen around you. You figure out how to let people know that She might come in and it's not your job or your business to stop Her.

As a Hierophant, this is much easier to do. Even mentorship can allow for this more easily than "teacher". But, if you are creative, you can include ways to let folks know how things might go.

The nature of the White Path is to truly, actively, be in the position of being Her mouthpiece to a degree the other paths really aren't. So you can imagine the degree of personal awareness, integrity, centeredness, and rooting one must have to do this well.

When She comes in, this is not carte blanche to behave in abusive or really weird ways. Nor are you let off the hook for the results of your role in this path.

As I've said, the path perpetuates itself. So fall-out will be a part of the initiatory process.

It's a strange thing to have a transmission come through and have it really mess someone up. Because they are not in relationship with Her the way you are, and because they can only see you as the source of the experience, you are, in the eyes of other people, responsible for what comes out of you.

The amount of maturity and skillfulness one must have to be the only visible, and viable, source of these transmissions is immense. Sometimes what comes out is so piercing, so potent, as to be brutal. Oftentimes the person through whom the transmission comes has no way of knowing how it will impact the person they are giving it to.

Just because a transmission tries to come through does not mean you need to allow it. Just because a transmission comes through does not mean you do not ask for permission to share it. Just because a transmission tries to come through does not mean you allow it without using discernment and engaging the other person in what's trying to happen.

White Path people are accountable for what they teach. White Path people are accountable for what they transmit. White Path people are accountable for the fall-out of being

Her mouthpiece. You can see how doing work to shift from independence to interdependence is necessary for this path. You can also see, even if it seems paradoxical, how essential personal accountability is.

Because each path cultivates us as vessels for Her to be in this world, and because deepening in this path transforms us into, ultimately, servants for her, and being how other people we encounter are likely to not be in the same kind of relational awareness of Her as we are, there is a certain inevitably to both blowing people's minds and of ruining lives. This is part of it. It's Savage.

Figuring out how to walk the White Path is brutal because of this. It requires, in my view, the greatest awareness, embodiment, understanding of humanness, and love because the White Path person becomes like a lightning strike. Potent, pure wisdom comes through with no other focus, not spirit-work, not sex or art, and not healing. It is pure transmission with no buffer. So we must learn to buffer or to set a container and to cultivate the ability to listen from a very deep place when we strike and leave versus when we strike and stay to help post-strike. This is Hierophant-level White Path.

The Hierophant is the final stage of the White Path before the Ocean of Initiation. Hierophants are those who interpret sacred mysteries or esoteric principles.

How this works is that the more you are "activated" in your role as vessel, and the more you learn how and what people need to truly learn, then the more you are able to be in the position of Hierophant.

This is because the very act of "interpreting" the sacred mysteries of esoteric principles means we take them from a kind of etheric state through our own understanding into "usable" or "accessible" forms.

The Hierophant is a kind of translator. But this translation happens, and makes it different from merely understanding and teaching what you understand, from a very deep and complex place - it happens from interdependence and maturity and all the things this path requires.

There are a lot of humans who can perceive, to a decent degree, sacred mysteries and esoteric knowledge. Most of them, however, use their heads to engage the revelations or insights they have. So they teach from their heads.

The Hierophant transmits the sacred into this world in a way that imbues it into the cells of another. The information tends to be distilled and simplified. Or it may be very mysterious and "out there" but simply being exposed to it will have a transformative or nourishing or disturbing impact on those who hear. A person who accesses sacred mysteries who is not a Hierophant tends to make the knowledge obscure, overly complex, and rather more a display of their brilliance than the holy gift it is.

The quality of any stage of any initiatory path is how the person feels to others. It is not how much you know or how powerful you are. It is the impact, the effect, your presence has on the life around you. This means that you are not *trying* to have an impact by pushing buttons or manipulating others. At least, not unless that is the sacred duty She has given you.

It means that no matter where you are, things will happen around you that are strange, even if you are just sitting there minding your own business.

This is because the deeper into these paths we go, the more of Her that emanates from us.

Part Five:

Three Phases of the Initiatory Path

Twenty-four

THREE PHASES OF THE INITIATORY PATH OVERVIEW

I know that orientation on this path is important - to have *some* sense of where you are, and maybe of where you aren't. And while it is a shifting and indefinite thing, we all need orientation. I have been providing orientation throughout this book for you. It is so crucial to this path. And now I want to share yet another form of it. This orientation is in our relationship to the initiatory path.

These three phases are about our awareness of, and relationship to, the path itself.

As you learn about this, please keep in mind that understanding will likely benefit you, but it will also help you to help others you might encounter. After all, She has a way of making it so that, at some point, the people most drawn to us are, themselves, on an initiatory journey. And since we are healers, teachers, artists, and witches, we encounter people who need our help or particular way of being in order to survive, or deepen, in their own journey.

Your being able to recognize someone's own relationship to Her, and to what is happening to them, can literally save a life. It can also ease pain and suffering, provide relief, and calm anxiety. Anxiety, depression, outsiderness, and disorientation are hallmarks of this path. So knowing as much as we can about the path helps us and helps those we encounter.

This book is filled with characteristics of this path. Many, I'm sure, you have identified you, yourself, as having. You have likely felt, at some point, oriented and, therefore, relieved, at having some understanding of a particular struggle or some relief at the sense-making that has happened for you at various points in these pages.

So this section is intended to provide more of that, but it may also be something that happens through you for other people. Though I do hope it helps you as well.

Each phase of our relationship to the initiatory path has its own challenges and hallmarks. This is what we are going to explore.

There are three phases of relationship with initiation and with the paths of the Dragon Mother:

1. Ignorant

2. Informed

3. Bound

The following three chapters explore each of these stages. Please read each one, even if you believe just one is more relevant to you, because each chapter has keys and wisdom that will augment how you navigate these waters, especially if you meet someone else who you suspect might be on this path who may need your help.

Twenty-five

IGNORANT

"Ignorant" is when we have no idea what is happening to us. When we "don't know what we don't know". In this stage we are noticing that there are some weird things going on, we are noticing our struggles that seem abnormal to other people's struggles, we are likely coming to awareness of the need to do some kind of healing or that we need support.

Ignorant is the "I'm struggling and aware that my struggling is harder or weirder or longer than it should be or is for others."

Ignorant can also mean "I am in crisis and don't know why and no one seems to be able to really explain to me what is going on".

This is the stage where many people begin to seek professional help. This means that this stage can be particularly vulnerable because, in a society that pathologizes pretty much everything, someone in this stage can get a diagnosis that, even if accurate, lacks the context that would allow the person diagnosed to truly understand what is going on and what to do about it.

I want to be clear - if you are in the initiatory path of the

Dragon Mother, medication and this path are not mutually exclusive. Therapy, medical help, or other conventional forms of treatment are not automatically invalid or to be avoided. She will use whatever context you are in and She can penetrate and exploit any situation you are in to communicate with you and guide you.

We want to be the best vessels possible for Her while still Being Where We Really Are. Sometimes medication helps us be that vessel and sometimes it gets in the way. It depends on the accuracy of our diagnosis, what other tools and means we have available, our maturity and experience with whatever condition we have, the supports we have, and how skillful we are with ourselves navigating day-to-day reality. Sometimes we need medical intervention because things don't need to be so hard for so long.

The clients who come to me who are ignorant of what's going on are almost always relieved to find out they are living the hallmarks of initiation. Having new frameworks and lenses through which to view themselves and their lives allows much needed reprieve and energy to come in. It is an exciting and also vulnerable time for many.

Because as the truth, as the resonance and possibility of initiation, sinks in, we also kind of have to face the truth of our otherness, our outsiderness, along with the daunting newness of the learning curve and, therefore, the *work* we have ahead of us. For many of us, we have already been working so hard that learning we have been working on things that are not the core thing can be daunting and defeating.

Many people can burst into tears at the idea that they really are freaks. Or feel grief that they have suffered for so long with no idea what was happening to them and with no help.

While this is ultimately good news and joyous, I understand that for many people it is very difficult and painful to swallow. Please keep this in mind should you be in a position of meeting one of Hers who is in this Ignorant stage. We want to be gentle and inviting and compassionate because of the ripple effect it can have in an individual's life to learn what is happening after what has potentially been such a long struggle.

Once someone kind of assesses how resonant or not the idea of being on an initiatory path is, they are going to have a lot of questions. If you are in this stage, you are going to have a lot of questions.

One of the most common is "What do I do now??"

The answer to this is "It depends".

- ❖ Are you waking up to the realization of initiation in the context of being a Christian who has diligently attended church and has grown increasingly dissonant and turned-off by the environment?
- ❖ Are you coming from a history of mental diagnosis and being pathologized?
- ❖ Are you coming from a scientism and rationalism background that says none of this is real?
- ❖ Have you spent your whole life masking and playing normal to try to fit in?

- ❖ Have you been slowly getting more and more ill and are exhausted?
- ❖ Have you fallen through the cracks your whole life and have just been lost?
- ❖ Have you built a life already and have a family and a job you fear you cannot rock the boat about?
- ❖ Have you been labeled and medicalized as "less than" in this ableist society and had your neurobiology or body pathologized?

I've worked with people in each of these situations. And there is no pat answer. Each person needs to be considered within their unique context and within the concerns they have. It's why I'm creating a sacred community online - so all us strange creatures have a community for support and education and tools we need to navigate our own individual waters within the greater path of belonging to Her.

Though each of us is in a unique situation, I think that starting an altar practice with the Ancestors is a pretty solid way to go. Kids love to participate in this, so if you have children, it's a great tradition to start. For those surrounded by Christians or other religious folk who are not pagan or otherwise not going to be okay with you deviating from their beliefs, lighting a candle for the recently dead or for the ancestors is pretty much always okay. You are honoring family. So a little altar somewhere in the home where you can do that has never, in my experience, been prevented, even in some pretty hard-core Abrahamic households.

The most important thing to keep in mind in this stage -

where one has been ignorant then had it revealed to them that they may be in an initiatory relationship with some Being - is that doing whatever they are cognitively, and experientially, able to do to get into relationship is what is most important. Because that opening, that reaching out to the one who has been reaching to us, that we belong to, enables Her to work with us in a way that we can more consciously recognize and receive. This allows things to begin to shift more potently, often with less struggle on our part.

It is also important that we do not try to say *who* the being is too soon. Many people walk this path and never have a "Patron Deity" experience. Within the pagan world the idea of a Patron Deity has been kind of made into some holy grail experience, like you have to find out who your patron deity is.

For those who truly belong to Her, She pulls people through their own ability to experience Her by meeting them in whatever they currently have available to them. This may look like Mary of the Christian world for some, Isis for others, Cernunnos for others, Odin or Kwan Yin, etc. No matter how real or how false a religion or belief may be, She will find a way to reach one of Her own through it.

When we are deep enough in this path, when we are transformed sufficiently, the traditions She appears through, the time and place and cultures She has revealed herself within, all drop away and become irrelevant. So the form we decide upon, the most ancient form of Her that we might take up, or perhaps the newest, is whatever we are most able to have intimacy and potency and devotion with.

It is not about her "truest" form, as if there is some "correct" one and the rest are false. It is about the form we are pulled into for whatever reason She pulls us there, for whatever reason She has for revealing and anchoring us in that aspect Being.

The main thing to consider is how we might be feeding, and perpetuating, the Field of Denial by some of the relational forms we choose to work with. I advise that people not do the very popular New Age thing of saying "all gods are one god so any god I choose is fine". We must be willing to discover by letting go of the human-created falsehoods, no matter how beloved they may be. It is the case that we often fear releasing the FOD placating we do by, say, conflating Mary of the Christian bible with Her.

If you are on this path, you will need to relinquish those false forms by learning to discern between human-created and actual Beings.

I do believe that those of us who are pulled into the Ocean of Initiation will absolutely encounter Her primal aspect and will experience the Great Serpent Androgyn. As with any of this path, how this might unfold is between you and Her and there is no goal other than to participate as best you can in Her hold on you and the FOD's grip fading, ever further, from your lived experience.

Twenty-six

INFORMED

The Informed stage is interesting. This is often where the early resonance and relief of discovery that occurs in the Ignorant stage gives way to the entrenched patterns and hyper-independence of the Field of Denial.

Informed is where we have seen and experienced the truth of our being on the initiatory path, yet we have not done enough to be sufficiently pulled from the FOD, to get into right-relationship, and to live as vessels for Her in this world.

People who are in the Informed stage often have the following characteristics:

- The urgency and relief of discovery gives way to complacency
- Doubt, rationality, and independence resurge
- Feeling inconvenienced by the requirements of relational reality
- Slipping into the idea that this path is somehow "optional"
- Starting an altar practice with some astonishing responses/results only to "forget" and go back to things as normal
- Believing it's not real and this is just crazy

- Slacking off on offerings and other things necessary for this path
- Feeling overwhelmed by their ideas about what it means if they really accept this and live this as a truth - i.e. they will "lose everything" or have no friends or be seen as even weirder
- Feeling overwhelmed by the juxtaposition between their New Age/Impersonal (i.e. "the universe") views and the relational intensity that arises as they open to Her
- Feeling "freaked out" or scared by how real this is - like it's not sock puppets in your head, your outer world begins to change in tangible, measurable, documentable ways that cannot be otherwise explained and folks get scared by that because they have been bombarded with the idea that this is not possible
- Fear that this is "evil"
- Fear that they are being "led astray" even when they profess to not be Chrisitan
- Backpedaling
- Trying to assert that they have choice like they are independent
- Overwhelmed by the rising sense of personal accountability that happens when one actually begins to feel the web of life

I could go on, but this is a pretty good smattering to give you some idea of what arises for folks in the Informed stage.

The Informed stage is, in essence, a territory with a lot of navigating and negotiating. It is the stage that carries the greatest challenges to our identities and beliefs.

In this stage it is **essential** that you make practice your main focus. By "practice" I mean that you begin to adopt new behaviors and modalities and give yourself the chance to have new experiences with different outcomes than the ones you have been accustomed to.

We do not transform via our thoughts, ideas, and beliefs. We transform by having lived experiences, different lived experiences, than we have heretofore had.

For many, these experiences will feel familiar - like "I used to do this as a kid" or I will suggest a practice to a client and they report they had already begun to spontaneously, and intuitively, do this. These kinds of things *go in your evidence journal.* It is crucial that you document the constant affirming, this-is-real things that happen so that the conditioned mind, the part of us that has been dominated by the FOD, can become liberated and awaken into the truth of Her and of what we actually are.

The Informed stage is also where we are most at risk for getting trapped in a power-trip - where we begin to get a little taste and feel, compared to others, of how enlightened or magical or deep or special we are. This is where we are most likely to get mesmerized by the "ooohs and ahhhs" of the sparkly magic show and lose connection to the realness of Her, this path, and of ecosystemic relationship. This is because the Field of Denial so values power that if we, unrooted and uncentered, experience the very normal miracle of belonging and becoming that is this path, may take that back to the Field of Denial as "proof" that we are powerful and want to exploit this for our own Less-Self gain.

The Informed stage is where we get a little taste of power, thinking it to be a huge amount of power, because compared to the flaccidity of the FOD it seems to be huge, and then we run with it. We might pronounce ourselves to be powerful Sorceresses or Priestesses or Sages or Gurus. In other words, this is the most likely stage for us to get really puffed-up and not even realize we are doing it.

What happens here is that we enter into a pocket reality *inside of* the FOD, believing ourselves to have become free of it, and then pronounce what this means about who and what we are. This always involves some sort of specialness that those in the FOD will eat up. We can make a ton of money, get acclaim, and be seen in the way our Less-Self prefers: as potent and special.

This doesn't mean there won't be magical experiences. This doesn't mean there won't be some power. This doesn't mean that nothing "true" or "helpful" comes from this space. But it does mean we have become tricked or hooked by the FOD and pulled back in. It fights to hold us. This is why a dedicated practice, even when we aren't "feeling it", is important. This is why rooting and centering in our bodies is important. This is why consistency is important. This is why putting Her first is important.

I know many people who have gone this way of the pocket reality. For many people, once they find this little pocket reality, the truth of their need for safety and specialness dominates and overrides relationship with Her and how

She wants to be in the world through us. Many will say this is Her work through them then they begin to lead people to archangels and loads of New Age stuff and never toward real embodiment or genuinely grounded ecosystemic spirituality or relational possibility - it's mostly sock puppets in their heads. Or it becomes about money.

This territory is tricky. Because none of us has any idea how or why She leads us as She does. So we can defensively say it's all Her to justify our motives. It's why I talk so much about being relational, and about experience and practice and rooting and the body and evidence journals and personal accountability. So much is necessary for us to work through so that we do not get lost again.

I am not going to profess to understand how She works. But I do know when someone slips into a pocket reality and claims they have some power and become gurus to others or use it for their gain. I know we all need money and comfort and ease to survive in this world. I want that for people. But there is wholeness and devotion and there is power-tripping and magical thinking that is not rooted in Her body.

Some people will say "But it's all Her so we are always on Her path". To that I say, stop head-fucking yourself. There is wholeness and belonging and relational reality and there is that which is capitulating to the FOD because we are unable to admit or deal with the very real fear and smallness we have. So we make ourselves special and divert attention from the Primal Reality and the necessity of being relational so we can be insulated instead.

This is valid.

It really is. You have the right to make that choice. But you must also have the integrity to own that this is the choice you are making and not play it off like something holy or magical or selfless. Like, go get that money. Get that security. Get that whatever you need at this place you are in, but do not lead others astray by playing that you are something you aren't, i.e. Her vessel/Priestess/Oracle.

What is so hard about this is that many people literally cannot see, or would even be willing to believe, that they have strayed - that their spiritual enlightenment or their power is pocket-reality-FOD stuff. This is why relationship is crucial. We must be rooted and oriented, IN OUR BODIES, and we must cultivate practices that tie us to Her, root us in relationship with Her, form spirit allies that guide and protect us, so that we can walk with humility, integrity, and devotion and not be caught up and distracted.

I mean *real* spirit allies. The problem with the Informed stage is that this is where the majority of our deeply entrenched psychological wounds dominate our landscape. This means we will see angels and believe we are channeling aliens or whatever, even have accurate predictions or some magical stuff happen, and never be able to tell we are not interacting with beings of the Unseen but are interacting with our own delusions or with aspects of the FOD.

Part of me feels a bit that the people this happens to don't actually belong to Her. But I think more of me believes it to simply be the power of the Field of Denial coupled with the situations we face as modern people. I know that I live with a certain idealism and I do not want that to obstruct or diminish the choices someone faces that I do not share. I am not here to gatekeep. I do, however, have decades of lived experience with this and I can tell you this territory is super tricksy.

So what we do is we couple Be Where You Really Are with as consistent of a practice as we can have with getting into right-relationship and learning and becoming, then meet whatever unfolds as best we can. I supposed if that means you become a New Age guru and make millions for 20 years and get people worshiping their own minds, then that's what it means. If you truly belong to Her, she will hold onto you. I would just hope that we resist the urge to use this as an excuse to not do what we can, as we can, to reach for Her. Even, and often, in spite of when our fears and needs tell us we must do otherwise - that we must do as the FOD would have us do.

I have such true compassion for the reality of how hard life can be for those of us that have been genuinely harmed. I understand how needed and necessary it can be to find pockets of reality where we are insulated from harm, even if that means living in a world of delusion.

For people who have been harmed in such deep ways, I would offer that you incorporate this into your work with Her, with Them, and let them know of your need for help, safety, insulation, and of your weakness. Not weakness like "pathetic", but weakness as in our smallness, our frailty, the truth of how harmed we can be living in bodies in a world that seeks to harm us whether through intent or negligence. We do well to admit our vulnerability and ask for help, instead of tucking it away inside of a kind of mind-trick we might create to deny that we are so frail. Our frailty is not a thing to be ashamed of, but a thing we must embrace if we are to ever truly understand what it means to be alive.

Twenty-seven

BOUND

Becoming bound happens in one of two ways:

1. We have been devoted to this path for some time and begin to see that we can no longer stray as far from it as we once could or
2. We realize we have always been bound to Her, that our entire lives have followed the breadcrumbs and calling and urgings of Her, and we finally accept this and live according to this truth

For many of us, as we begin to outgrow the Informed stage, becoming Bound happens as we start to see that what once was optional no longer is. We begin to connect the dots between our practice/devotion and how well, or not, our lives seem to work. We see correlates between honoring Her and this path and how well things go for us and how much things begin to fall apart and not work when we do not honor what we are.

Whether it is drinking too much alcohol or only occasionally going to our altar or engaging in things that are not aligned with wholeness and belonging, we begin to notice that those things seem to have a higher cost or take a greater toll. We begin to see that these things actually cause disruptions - disruptions that we actually do not care for.

Please do not do the thing where one takes a sentence like "drinking too much alcohol" and turns this into some kind of taboo or rule. Perhaps your path involves drinking more alcohol than another person's path. Who knows? Let's leave the puritanical gaze out of this.

In the Informed stage, our desires and Her desires are not super aligned. Indeed, the Informed stage is a place where we begin being attuned more and more to Her and to what we are.

In the Bound stage of relational awareness, we turn ever-increasingly to the relief of surrendering into Her - into our own unraveling and disappearance. This is the place where the individual self begins to hold less and less fascination and belonging comes to the fore. We come to experience that we are a multiplicity and we begin to feel joy and meaning primarily in relationship to Her.

As we are Bound, we begin to have realizations. These realizations arise from a self that takes meaning and fulfillment from service, a self that finds freedom from its place as Her vessel, Her voice, Her servant. As being Bound comes to fruition, the self relaxes into the body of Her, into our role, into releasing the need to know and control and figure out and dictate.

Interestingly, this is also the place where we begin to use our voice. This is the place where we shift from passive concepts of submission that we have been indoctrinated with into inclusion. What I mean is that we experience our own holiness just the same as we experience the holiness of all of life. We experience our needs and desires and real self as something not to be wrestled with and controlled or changed, but as something to be honest about.

For example, if you are very much a Red Path person, you may have been called into the vessel of Sacred Prostitute, where you are a channel for love and healing through a path of sensuality and sexuality that your Less Self benefits little from but that the person on the receiving end of is greatly touched by.

When you become truly Bound *and* are transformed through your feral devotion to this path, you might see that your truth is that you do not wish to be the Sacred Prostitute. You may see that you wish your body and heart to be in service to you and your own need and desire for a sacred beloved to share your life with. So you tell Her. You tell the Deeper Powers that you no longer wish for this and you want something else instead. You speak this from a place of truth, not dictate, but of respect *as one who belongs to, and speaks on behalf of, the ecosystem.*

This doesn't automatically mean you get what you ask for.

The way we are vessels for her changes and grows as we change and grow. The self that derives joy and growth and insight from loving in the way the Sacred Prostitute does may not be a self you always are.

Then again, you may always be a Red Path Sacred Prostitute and it may always fulfill you and be a way of being that you always learn and grow within.

Again, we always practice, and return to, Be Where You Really Are. It serves us, always.

Being Bound is walking with deep respect for yourself. This path is holy and such an honor to be transformed in this way for Her. It takes so much for us to walk it.

While I do not take credit for what She does through me, for what She teaches me, for what She shows me, and for the powers she opens and enables in me, I absolutely do take credit for what this path has required of me and the choices I have made, the courage I have shown, the sheer determination I have, the fearlessness and badassery that lives in me, my refusal to give in to the Field of Denial, my endless thirst for understanding, and the sweetness of my innocent heart. (I also give my mom credit for demonstrating and cultivating this for me.)

Being bound is where life becomes inclusive, whole, ecosystemic, and where justice and Her view dominate our own lenses. So we use our voice for ourselves not because we are "empowered", but because the holiness of life is alive in us. We begin to speak out on behalf of the self because the Less Self has disappeared so much at this point that we experience ourselves as a part of the greater reality much as we experience a bird or a human child or a tree. We are no more but we are no less and we do not take the fact of our holiness personally.

You see how we move, always move, away from binaries and linearity and extremes and into wholeness and relationship? You see where otherness disappears into the ocean of belonging? You see where the lenses of the FOD dissolve into irrelevancy?

What pathology? What shame? What guilt? What morality?

When we are Bound, these things become difficult to find in our living bodies.

When we become Bound, we enter the terrain within our own felt sense of what we are in a way that disestablishes the FOD unreality. Our vision changes. The layers of dissociation and disconnection slide off of us like water on oil. And we are left with the Innocent Self revealed to us, and revealing to us the secret truths of Her fierce and holy Being.

The journey of being Bound to Her is an ever-increasing transformation into a self that is a multiplicity - a self that cannot say where it ends and any other life begins - a self that cannot say, with any sliver of truth, that the bird and the tree and itself are truly separate.

Please understand that I am not saying "All is One". For this is no more true than "All is Separate". Neither of these exist in the Primal Realm, that realm that is rife with paradox that is utterly free of tension about it.

We must be aware that the examples most of us have of any of this kind of stuff that I am speaking to here is from Western interaction with Buddhist thought, Christian notions, and New Age thought.

Be careful to not overlay these expectations onto this path. Be careful that you do not start to perform your version of "service" or "devotion" or "sacred".

The Dragon Mother is the Eater of Filth. She dwells, too, where rotting corpses and shit and murderers dwell. She is not immune to any place or aspect of life, nor does she prohibit them.

What She wants from you, with you, is between you and Her. If She wants you to immerse yourself in Death, you shall. If She wants you to immerse yourself in sex work, art, sacrifice of your own life force for another, rescue work, immersion in study, necromancy, divination, or any other millions of things She may require of you, you shall if you are Bound.

What I am pointing to here is that no one can know your walk with her. There are those of us who are familiar enough with Her that we can feel when She is present versus a Field of Denial trickster. But, ultimately, *you are responsible* for cultivating the ability to root, center, and know Her. You are responsible to cultivate what you must to earn right relationship and spirit allies, to enter dream space so you may speak with Her or others to gain guidance and answers, to become truly *Witched* so that you do transform into one so bound that you become Her hound in this life, her dog, serving Her and taking joy and meaning from your life as Hers.

For some of you reading this, especially if you are not near this stage of your relationship with Her, this chapter may feel abhorrent, offensive to your FOD sensibilities, keenly unpleasant to your hyper-independence. It may assault your Christian indoctrination, your New Age mind-fuckery, your Scientism.

What I know is that you are either on this path, or you are not. You may not be ready for these things right now, but one day these words here may save your life, or your sanity. If you have not already closed this book and walked away, perhaps you *do* belong to Her. Only you can know, and it may take this entire lifetime to be sure, there is that much baggage and nonsense for us all to wade through.

I can tell you that the experience of being Bound is a mutually beneficial existence. We are not martyrs. We are not slaves. What we are is shifting from one way of being into *becoming in each moment a lived responsiveness to life that is rooted in Her body within the incomprehensible vastness of the web of life through our own bodies, right now and now and now and now and now.*

Anything else is a falsehood we do well to put effort into losing our fascination with and our need of.

Perhaps your being has a glimpse of what this means? Perhaps you sense that being Bound to Her is living in a way that means we do not try to make sense of anything, only that we sense this life, that we care for the health of the ecosystem and the many beings in it, that the sacred unfolding happens as it is meant to and that we participate in that as She directs, and lives through, us.

Being Bound means we stop resisting the truth that we are inextricably a part of this life, that we matter no more or no less than any other life, that we wish to be alive and safe like any other life, that human morality and Primal Reality are often vastly different and we work to hold the paradox of our tiny human needs in the vastness of Her acting through us and not have our heads pop because of the impossibility of it when we are still too enmeshed with the FOD.

Our work is to reach for Her. The rest unfolds as it will. The Less Self *hates* this.

Part Six:

The Unseen Realm

Twenty-eight

THE UNSEEN REALM OVERVIEW

The Unseen Realm is something each of us must find our own place for in how we experience the world. In this day and age it is very common to refer to the forces of this world in generic and impersonal terms. Things like "The Universe" and "Spirit" and "energy" as impersonal ways of relating to what we know is a greater kind of Intelligence present in our lives.

The Unseen Realm can be known in many ways. But our approach should always be one that is relational, as if these beings are real - not ideas or concepts or archetypes or patterns. They *are* real. As real as you or me or the earth beneath your feet.

Being real and being knowable are two different things, however. Something being knowable means we have access to it. Gaining access to the Unseen is different from belief.

Just as you may want to know someone more personally, there are relational things required to gain this kind of intimacy with a person.

The Unseen realm is that aspect of reality that is not readily visible or available to us. It is mysterious and strange. It functions via different physics than our visible realm. And the beings there do as well.

How your particular culture and family speaks about, and conceptualizes, and has folklore about, the Unseen is as varied as there are cultures. So your study and endeavors to learn what you can in the ways you are drawn are essential. Entire books have been written about what this realm is, so a couple of chapters in a book on Initiation isn't going to adequately give you the depth of understanding you will need for this path.

You need to research. You need to put in effort to seek Them out. You must take leaps of faith and cross FOD boundaries that say the Unseen isn't real and the beings of the Unseen are evil or bad or to be avoided.

I think that most of us are born with an innate sense of the aliveness in all things. I think many of us have a sense of other beings that do not appear in common vision. We encounter beings in the dream realm. We are whispered to in the dark. We are guided and kept from harm in strange and mysterious ways. We are also messed with and sometimes harmed by things that we can, after enough torment, only describe as having the sense there is a being behind it, like an energy parasite or evil entity.

The Chrisitan lens calls this possession. Or demonic forces - where "demonic" means "evil", having erased the original "daemon", which simply means any being of the Unseen, with "demon", making all of the Unseen evil, except things like "angels" or things "of God".

While I would never claim the beings of the Unseen are benign, it serves us to untangle ourselves from a lens of good/evil. Good and evil promote ideas of safety and danger. They make us seek the good and avoid the evil, which serves to antagonize wholeness. It also serves to keep us locked in the Less Self and reliant on the Field of Denial. This reliance is for the *illusion of immunity* and does not serve to actually protect us much from the Greater Reality, which includes the Unseen Realm.

The Unseen Realm does not "make sense". No matter how familiar we become with it, it will always have elements of the unknowable, the wild, the erratic, and the dangerous. It is not a realm we can control or command. It does not follow rationalism, logic, rules, or scientific exploration.Nor does it conform to what Chrisitians might say about it.

What we can learn are the ways that we might traverse the territory, and interact with the Beings of the Unseen, to gain the good regard of those beings. Much of the history of magic and sorcery has to do with learning how to stay protected from, journey in, and engage with this realm.

In the next chapter I am going to share some basics that I have shared with my clients, and in some of my classes, that set a nice foundation for working with the Unseen.

Twenty-nine

WORKING WITH THE UNSEEN

Each one of us will discover different ways to work with the Unseen. Some of us have naturally been doing it since we were kids. Others will be taught by mentors. And others will read about it in books, be taught through dreams, or simply make it up as they go and see what works. There are all kinds of ways one might learn.

Over the years, I've developed a foundational formula, if you will, that anyone can begin to use. If you are further along your path, perhaps something here will be useful. If you are new or new-ish (say less than 3 years in), what follows should serve as a lovely foundation for you that you, and the spirits, will build upon or tweak, or move past in good time.

Many people who are new to the concept of working with the Unseen feel apprehensive or downright scared. We have been bombarded with concepts of dangerous spirits and demons since we were born. We have been taught it is evil, dark, bad, or immoral to engage with such things.

While I am not going to tell you it is safe, and I'm certainly not going to tell you there aren't dangers, I will say that there *are* ways to begin that can give us a good start. If you already have ways you practice, perhaps read this chapter anyway? I've worked with a lot of people who were taught wrong or who were getting messed with because they were engaging in ways that were problematic or ignorant.

As a society, we have gotten so far removed from working with the Unseen in any kind of relational way that none of us should be ashamed or feel bad about any mistakes we've made. Many of us are making it up as we go and doing our best. Heck, I tried summoning a demon when I was 16 out of a "satanic book" because it was all I could get my hands on back then. We work with what we have and most of us have no concept of how real these beings are until we are affected, positively or negatively, by them.

As a general rule of thumb you might start working with either spirits of place or ancestors. I typically start people off with an ancestor practice. Even if your dead relatives were horrible people when alive you can start an ancestor practice. This is because you can call to the ancestors you specify. All of us have both well and unwell ancestors. You can call to the ones that you feel the safest with. We all have good ancestors somewhere in our lines.

Our ancestors are some of the only spirit beings who have what we might call a vested interest in our well-being. We have blood ties to them. We have history and imprints from many of them. For some of us, our bodies were made from the same land as their bodies we made.

Now, at some point everyone wants to know about what spirits really are and what "rules" there are with them. Like "If spirits aren't really people anymore, but conform more to the ways of the Unseen than to this realm, then what am I talking to? How does this work?"

The best thing I can say to anyone working with spirits is:

a) learn from experience - let them reveal themselves to you and teach you and

b) do your research and explore the history of what other humans have learned about them - start with your own cultural roots or wherever you feel initially drawn.

I do not care for fussy things. So my approach to most things, including my spiritual path, is not-fussy. I have always been a dive-in-and-discover kind of person and I believe the best way to learn about spirits is from spirits themselves. Having said that, I do think there is a way to approach this that gives a bit of orientation and smart start that can work for most people. And that's, as I said, an ancestor practice.

It has been my experience that ancestral spirits tend to be fairly responsive in fairly undeniable ways, fairly quickly. Most of my clients have gotten responses within a couple of weeks or less. More often it's a day or three.

What do I mean by responses?

It can be anything, really. But it's usually odd events that are related to the beginning of an ancestral practice. I once had a client who started a practice and felt called to her great, great aunt so reached out to her and made offerings, then received a box of her possessions the very next day that she didn't even know was in the family that her sister somehow had that she was about to donate to Goodwill.

They have ways of making themselves known to us. But it is through relationship with them that we make this communication most viable.

But how, exactly, do we do that?

There is a saying, and I cannot remember where I learned this, but it is: I give so that you may give.

What I have learned from meditating on this saying while at my altar, in the presence of my own ancestors, is that our giving of substance from this world gives them what they need to have an effect in this world. "...so that you might give" is that they *want* to give to us, to support and help and guide us, and that they need us to make that possible through our offerings.

Giving is essential in any community or relational capacity. The Elder Futhark rune Gebo is about exchange - specifically about the kind of exchange that obligates us to one another in a perpetual cycle that is at the foundation of community. You borrow sugar from me, I give you some of the pie I made with. I borrow your lawn mower then mow your lawn while I'm outside mowing my own as a thanks and contribution back to you.

This kind of giving-that-obligates is a good and necessary thing. And when we do this with good will and a lack of manipulation, we are, indeed, on our way to right-relationship.

So we give to our ancestors and the spirits.

I think of the fact that they have been giving to us our whole lives and, for many of us, we have been unaware of this and, consequently, have never really made offerings. So, in a way, we could give daily for the rest of our lives and it would be small compensation for all that we have received.

I have found, as have many of my clients, that when we first call, and make an offering, to our ancestors that there is a palpable feeling of joy. What I mean is there is a feeling of *their* joy at being remembered and honored and fed. It is humbling and gentle and profound.

So giving is the foundation. Indeed, it is the foundation of *any* relational work you do with spirits. The Dragon Mother gets a regular meal every month on the new moon from me. You might want to consider implementing a practice like this, however you may know Her.

So here is a basic, and simple, formula for you to consider that will be more than sufficient to begin a legitimate ancestor/spirit practice:

1) Have a dedicated space. This can be as simple as a handkerchief on a dresser or as elaborate as you would like. You can fit an altar pretty much anywhere.

2) Do something simple like lighting a candle that is for your ancestors.

3) Craft a "call". The Call is what you say to specifically call

to the ancestors you would welcome contact with. I recommend people start back, where relevant, before Chrisitan colonization of their indigenous ancestors. We all have indigenous ancestors in our lines. For many of European descent, we often need to go back 1000 years or more.

4) Have some kind offering: a song, a poem you wrote, incense, whiskey, apples, tea, even a glass of water offered with a sincere heart.

5) End it there or speak to them. Tell them what is on your heart.

6) Thank them and say "we will talk again _____" (i.e. "tomorrow" or "next Sunday") Consistency is important with this. So if you can reliably make it only once a week, that is okay, but you need to show up. "I give so that you may give" isn't just about offerings. It's about our time and dedication and effort.

7) Keep an Altar Journal. This is where you spend a few moments writing the date and whatever transpired - like "I gave offerings and then shared with them _____. I asked for _____. I promised _____. I heard _____. I was taught _____."

Let's drill down on a few key points.

Crafting a Call: You are going to find one or two words that encapsulate the ancestors you are wanting contact with. Like, I say "Ancestors of might and magic" because might, to me, encapsulates not only physical vitality, but also integrity, character, and will. I say magic because I want the witchy, tuned-in, sorcerously potent, herb-y, rune-reading, animal-talking, tree-listening folk in my line.

So crafting the call is who you wish to connect with and, by omission, who is not welcome or being called to. If you do not feel the need to leave anyone out but want to make offerings to all of your ancestors for whatever reasons you may have, craft the call to reflect this. Your own wisdom and feelings should guide you.

Offerings: Look into traditional offerings in your lineage. Think about what your recent dead folk liked in life - coffee or a beer or Frank Sinatra music. Think about what you have on hand. Listen for what you feel an instinct for and don't let your head get in the way.

We want our offerings to be nourishing and sustaining - so we want them to have *life force* in them. Traditional offerings in my own ancestry include cream, cheese, butter, whiskey, ale, fatty meat, eggs, nuts, fresh fruit, flowers. As I am mostly Scandinavian, labor is also much appreciated - meaning I will clean my kitchen and dedicate this labor. I will keep my house well as an ongoing offering and respect to Them. One of my clients loves to sing and will use her voice for offerings and they are quite potent and loved.

Speak to Them: This is a time to share what is truly on your heart. Do not let the "they aren't really real" or "they can't help me" or "I don't want to burden them" get in your way. Truly tell them what your life is like. Tell them where you struggle and need support. Tell them what talents or strengths you have that you are grateful for. Tell them how your other living relatives are and ask for their support and protection of these people (or for their correction if you have some dysfunctional family members). You may be surprised when tears flood from you as your burdens are lifted from your shoulders because your ancestors step in to share the load with you.

Altar Journal: An Altar Journal not only helps you track and remember sessions and what you shared, it serves as an Evidence Journal. What I mean is that you will be told things at your altar that you have no way of knowing that you will later discover are quite significant. Like I used to get told things in other languages, specifically Old Norse, Scottish, and Welsh - none of these languages I remotely speak - as answers to questions I had. Like If I asked for insight I might get told a word in some language and I'd write it down as best I could then would go google translate it, only to find it was exactly the answer to the thing I asked.

Having a record of this allows our conditioned mind to begin to relax into the veracity of these beings and these relationships. The hyper-rational mind of scientism and modernity will not be able to stand in the face of the accumulation of undeniable actual events that occur, making the relational nature of the spiritual path blossom in our bodies and lives. It is necessary and empowering.

The Altar Journal also allows you to track things you ask for and promises you make.

One tip: If you make a promise, put it in your modern calendar so you can track, and fulfill, the promise. In other words, integrate this work into your modern life using modern means.

Consistency: SHOW UP. Decide how often you can come and, when you do your first altar session with your ancestors, tell them how often you will come. Then do it. Consistency is incredibly important. As with any relationship, you keeping your word and being consistent builds trust and connection. You are not simply "doing altar work", you are meeting with beings that are important to you. Show them the same respect and honor you would any living human you deeply care for.

Now I am going to share with you my own entire ancestor practice so you can get an idea of how this might look:

I sit down to my altar and light the charcoal I will use for the incense. I have three candles I use. I light the first candle and say "I light this candle in remembrance of my ancestors." I light the second candle and say "I light this candle in honor of the Disir." I light the third, center candle, and say "Hail Hela for caring for my ancestors."

Then I do the Call by saying "I kneel before you now with spoken prayers to say. Ancestors of might and magic, I ask that you hear my words. May the doors between our worlds open so that we may see, know, and touch one another across space and time."

Then I give an offering of incense and say "Ancestors, accept this offering. Though your names and deeds may have been lost to time, you yourselves are not, for you live on in me and I am here and I remember you, I honor you, and I love you."

Then I tell them the day, the date, and the season and what the weather is doing. For example "Ancestors, it is Wednesday the 5th of April in the year 2023. It is spring. It's cold and wet today but the birds are chirping like mad! There are yellow daffodils everywhere. And frogs chirping. And the field is so green. I have been tilling the soil in the garden to get it ready for seeding."

Then I say whatever I have to say or ask whatever I need to ask.

I give more incense. I may give a small meal or some whiskey or brandy.

Then I snuff out each candle with a candle snuffer in the reverse order of how I lit them and, as I do I say "Hail Hela. Hail the Disir. Hail my Ancestors. We will talk again tomorrow."

Then I write in my altar journal and am done.

As my practice has evolved over these many decades, my focus is now primarily on my path with the Dragon Mother. I do give offerings to my ancestors, but it is no longer a daily thing at my altar. I have woven my offerings to them into my day.

Your practice will evolve and change. So will your altar. Do not get hung up on there being a right way. This is organic and unfolding and we are all learning and experiencing and doing different as we know different.

I am frequently asked if I have different altars for different things I do. I do not. I cannot handle fussy or overly complex things to manage. I have one altar and an entire wall with things like images, deer skull, hawk wing, and jewelry all with a bookcase for my witchy books and tons and tons of herbs and potions and incense and such. It is comfortable with pillows on the floor for me to sit and all of my divination and altar tools for easy access for whatever I might need. My altar journals and pens are there as well. I also use the space outdoors for offerings and sitting-out journeys and such.

Anywhere you are can be an altar. But creating dedicated spaces do, over time, become extremely potent.

You can also carry offerings around with you. Many times we might be out in the world and find ourselves someplace where an offering or a prayer or something for an exchange might be necessary. Perhaps a yew tree you were not expecting whose needles you use in a smoke might need an offering if it gives you permission to take some of its body? Perhaps a spot of whiskey on land that has been disrespected with some tobacco and a prayer to the spirits of place? We never know when we might need a bit of tobacco or a coin and it is good to have these things on you as you go about your day.

As you work with spirits, you will find that you get nudges and urges and will become increasingly equipped for the work. Don't be too in your head about it. Get to know them and they will participate in your path.

You will find that the Dragon Mother has many guises,

allies, and many reasons for her various forms. What we must do is work to become devoted and consistent so that we may deepen with Her.

In the next chapter I am going to address the apprehension many folks have shared with me that they have about having a spirit practice and address some of the most common concerns that arise from the unknowing and the fear about the spirit realm and spirits in general.

Thirty

FEAR, EVIL, AND NAVIGATING THE UNKNOWN

Nearly every single person I have worked with, witchy or not, has concerns about getting involved with spirits.

The first concern is usually about the danger of it, as if they will instantly be attacked by evil or harmful spirits.

Throughout your walking of the initiatory path you are going to encounter multiple ways in which the conditioning of the Field of Denial must be confronted and addressed. Working with spirits just so happens to be one of the deeper ones.

For all our rational, scientific modernism, many folks just plain fear that there is something evil about working with spirits. People will tell you they don't feel that way, yet still "surround themselves with white light" and pray to archangels or otherwise feel the need to protect themselves from what lurks in the dark.

I'm not about to say that there are not things that will harm you.

But conflating dark with evil, and spirits with "avoid", is definitely Field of Denial indoctrination.

As with every single thing I've said in this book, you need to have your own experiences. This is why starting with Ancestral Work is a good start. Not because ancestors are fundamentally safer, but because they are safer for an indoctrinated mind. We have, all of us, been indoctrinated to some degree in the Western world. It's just that few of us witchy folks realize how deep the indoctrination goes because we haven't "belonged" in conventional ways, or we've always had some layer of insulation, like our innocence or strange brains, from the FOD.

This doesn't make us immune and it can, in fact, make us naive about how much of that which we do not even hold true actually has us by the short-hairs.

Walking this path requires that you form relationships with the beings of the Unseen. Further, and I want this to be completely clear, it means having relationships with the Unseen on its own terms, on Her terms, and not with the buffers and insulation of the Field of Denial.

Yes, this means you do not pray to Jesus to stay safe when you go out in the dark woods on a full moon. But it means so much more.

Walking this path means you form relationships with the strange beings of the Unseen that serve to keep you safe. In other words, you become safe because you are in right-relationship and have earned, and learned, how to be where you are and how to walk this path, *not* because you have some delusional "buffer" the Field of Denial has created.

Walking this path is learning to align with power-filled allies of the Unseen - not insulating yourself from it while you try to walk around in it. This is a vital shift in framing and behavior.

Further, for many people who have been on this path for a while and have worked with the Unseen, they are shocked or thrown when they have gone from the FOD into Limbo and are coming through Limbo and then, finally, begin to encounter the real deal with the Unseen.

Like you've had nature spirit experiences, ghosts, curses, and rich ancestral relationships and you think that's what this is. Then you really break free of the grasp of the FOD and are required to deepen. This is the territory of predator/prey, Primal Reality.

This is where the Unseen begins to show itself more and you encounter beings that look very strange and, often, terrifying (to the FOD mind).

This is when you feel spirits sit on your bed, breathe on your neck, talk with you in your dreams, introduce themselves.

This is when you learn to make pacts (agreements), learn to work with powerful beings that are dangerous because of their power and place that, if approached well, will actually protect you from more dangerous spirits.

Why you might need to do this is not the purview of this book. There are many, many reasons She may pull you this deep. But, rather than leave you guessing or fearful, I will say this:

As we are Her hands and hearts and eyes and mouths in this world, we see and feel and are exposed to the egregious injustices and the many sick predators who destroy and imbalance the many lives around them. One human, even many humans, within human systems, can do woefully little even with concerted, exhausting effort. But one human with powerful spirit allies can restore balance or bring down a predator quite readily.

We are not here for ourselves.

Initiation isn't so we can feel good and special. There is work to be done. There is a world on fire that needs to be tended. And She tends to it through us. We must become what we need to be for Her to do that work. This means working within ecosystemic reality, guided by Primal Intelligence, working through, and within, human beings and the many realities we create that assault ecosystemic health and belonging. Even in the absence of the FOD and its atrocities, She still has human vessels and that has been true throughout all time and will always be true. Every single thing is Her body.

As I have said in many different ways throughout this book, you must make your own way according to what She wants with you. So I don't know what you will learn and encounter differently from what I have learned and encountered. I've seen some pretty intense things that would scare the crap out of most people. I've been places that would drive many mad. I've encountered beings that are legitimately menacing. And each of those encounters were guided by spirit allies who got me through.

Spiritual-ecosystemic reality is vastly different than the FOD. You must enter into it, learn and function according to it, in order for it to be safe. This is the same with *any* culture different from your own. This does not make it evil, just potentially dangerous if you barge in with arrogance and ignorance. Arrogance and ignorance can get you harmed anyplace.

So the fear that arises, and it will, is something to be attentive to. The way you are attentive to it is by recognizing the FOD stories that fill your every cell and scream delusional nonsense at you from every Christian tale of demons to every scary movie you've seen to all the socially normative rejection and demonizing of Primal Reality that is woven into our day-to-day realities.

The Field of Denial has been waging war against Primal Reality and your body and mind are the battlefield. Our "innate" fear and reviling of it are the proof. *Especially* in those of us who are born to this path - that we are still so tentative and scared and worried to take the necessary steps to get closer to Her - that we fear "evil" and "demons" and that this is fundamentally bad.

So much of what takes place for us on this path occurs in the private interiority of it. What I mean is that we have these strange, miraculous experiences, these "proofs" that there *is* something there, that this *is real,* but it happens privately. However, when you are far enough on this path, when you have become strange enough, when you have seen and experienced enough and your evidence journal is chock full of the veracity of Her and of the Unseen, things are no longer private and what is required of you is no longer some small thing you can tuck into and out of.

No, this path permeates everything. And the deeper you go, the more of Hers you are, the stranger and stranger things will happen around you, and be required of you.

So there is a threshold you will come to. That threshold is the place of staying, or leaving, the realm of morality. That threshold is the place of staying in the FOD's grasp on you or in choosing to live according to Primal Intelligence and Its rules and ways.

There is no safe initiation. There is no comfortable initiation. There is no halfway initiation. There is no playing priestess or witch on weekends or in private. There is no being part this and part that. If you belong to Her and this path, you must do everything in your power to extract the FOD's tentacles and all its particulates from your cells. All while living with the truth of modern life - that you are immersed in modernity, that the roots of your blood have likely been severed, or wounded, that just your existence as a modern person causes harm to the ecosystems you are a part of. You must master Paradox to walk this path.

Navigating the Unknown takes time. The more you work with spirits, the more you learn, the more you behaviorally enact relationship and belonging, the easier it will be to face the things you must face and do the things you must do.

As I have said, this path undoes us. This isn't a poetic statement. This is truth. We *must* become undone so that we can be the multiplicity we are in this complex web of life. We must be able to be transformed from a self to a system so that the unknown doesn't freak us out *because* we are capable of intelligent responsiveness beneath the level of the conscious mind - *not* because we "know" things.

In other words, your ability to navigate the Unknown is not by knowing in the way we are taught to know, but in being capable of allowing Deeper Intelligence to work through you, to arise and respond through you in any given moment, allowing the belonging and your place in the ecosystem and wider web to play out according to ancient wisdom and ecosystemic need. In the FOD perspective, this is not only impossible and foolish, but scary as hell. The FOD is full-stop anti-becoming-undone; it is anti-belonging to Primal Intelligence.

This bears repeating: The Field of Denial is anti-belonging to Primal Intelligence.

In other words, the Field of Denial is anti-Dragon Mother. Said another way, the Field of Denial is anti-life. It is against *what life is.* And our entire lives have been an immersion in that anti-life field. Our entire lives have been fear and rage and ignorance and reviling and propaganda against the Deeper Intelligence that permeates all things. We have all been denied access to this Intelligence in ourselves and have been taught to believe that knowledge and power lie outside our own bodies in some way that is attainable to only the few in a way that is elusive and exclusive. In other words, it is gate-kept rather than innate.
I'm telling you here and now, it is innate.

I'm also telling you that the work required to live this innate belonging, power, and Intelligence that is an arising responsiveness is intense. How blessed are we to be taken up in the Initiatory current of Her? How mind-blowing is it that we have not been torn from Her? How profound and beautiful it is to contemplate the indisputability of our belonging? It is worth immersing yourself in. Let it into your cells.

Please know that your fear is a vital part of your transformation. And navigating the territory and content of your fear is an essential part of this path. It *is* part of the path, not some obstacle on it. Embrace this and go forward. Embrace this and be freaked out and confront that. Fear holds the possibility of a most potent transformation.

We are instilled with the fear that anything that is not Field-of-Denial-sanctioned is "evil". As always with this path, we must learn *what is* through our own, and trusted others', experiences.

The meaning, the opportunity, behind this is that we come ever more into reality as we leave behind stories and fears and patterns that are anything other than aligned with *what is.* The Dragon Mother, that ancient, primal being that is in and through and beneath all, dwells beyond constructs, lives within myth, and meets us ever-increasingly as the constraints of our conditioning are undone.

Do not be mistaken, She can, and will, use any construct we create to grab hold of us - nothing can hold Her back - for everything is Her body. The work we do is for us to be able to experience Her more readily, to experience the true nature of existence more readily, and to experience belonging as our natural home.

The Field of Denial is not our natural home. The Field of Denial seeks, vehemently, to keep us from the greater field of belonging. It does this by instilling us with fear and powerlessness and threat of annihilation if we leave. It says She is the great enemy and that it will protect us from Her.

Without coming to know Her beyond our fear and conceptions, how can we stand rooted in any truth whatsoever? We choose to invest in what will "keep us safe" because we have not grown our capacity for what life is, we have not ventured beyond the prison walls of the FOD, and we have not allowed the curious aliveness in us to breathe.

The opposite of fear is not courage. The opposite of fear is to dance the song that sings you and to rejoice in the complex melody of this holy life. Fear is one note in the symphony. There is so much more if we would but dare to allow ourselves to experience it.

What you seek seeks you. Extend your hand into that holy darkness.

Part Seven:

Tidbits, Tools, and Tips

Thirty-one

TIDBITS, TOOLS, TIPS OVERVIEW

This section has some thoughts that didn't logically fit anywhere else but that are common enough questions I get that I am going to pop them in here. This includes when people ask how to deal with the pressure and confusion of the initiatory experience.

So I've included a short introduction to the Four Pillars, some more words on being *witched,* and some other things I hope will aid your journey.

As this is the final section of this book, please allow me to take a moment to say a few words about this journey.

I hope I have made the necessity of our own deconditioning clear, as well as how tricky and arduous this is. I hope I have made it clear that the best way to proceed, indeed, the only real way to make it through this initiatory journey, is to form relationships with the beings of the Unseen - that they can, and will, teach and guide you far more wisely and well than any human could. This does not mean we should not seek out humans who have gone before us that might help us better navigate this path, we absolutely should.

I have sought out truly strange souls to help me on this

path and have, as I am sure you have, or will, utilized and incorporated what works for me, tried out many things that I later utterly discarded, and learned enough to begin to create my own practices, methods, and ways. It has always been like this. This path is a living path. We learn and grow and modify or invent as a part of the relationship. The past has much to teach, and we are wise to look to it, but the past comes from people whose minds and hearts we no longer understand because we live so differently.

There is a way to walk this path that honors lineage, the Spirits, ancestry, past knowledge, current teachers, and our own responsive arising, without appropriation or disregard or blatant acceptance of the things we encounter. This is trial by fire, yes, but it is also trial by error, education, and effort. You *will* learn. But that requires you to try.

So try. Try the things I suggest. Find other people whose work and words and spirit you relate to, all while rooting and centering as central practices so that you may cultivate discernment of your own and be guided by Them that are close to you.

This book is filled with suggestions and insights from decades of my experience with thousands of people. I have seen what works, what gets results, and what traps are in the path. Not all of this will be true or "work" for all people. But what is here *is* foundational and will lead you to making your own strange way.

Try what is written here. And remember that you will be both terrified and utterly amazed along the way. What you do with those feelings will, I hope, be informed by ever-increasing rooting, centering, devotion, and trust. A healthy touch of madness will aid you, as well.

Thirty-two
THE FOUR PILLARS

Some many years ago I devised a way for people to assess not only where they are struggling, but also determine what they might need to shift out of struggling. It is a model I created that exists utterly outside of pathology. In other words, it's helpful in figuring out what you need without making you "wrong" or "wounded" or "lacking consciousness" or infantile or whatever in the process.

I call this model The Four Pillars.

This will be a brief explanation of the Four Pillars that should be sufficient for you to utilize on your initiatory journey, yes, but also in any area - professionally, personally, relationally, with your children, in therapy, etc.

The Four Pillars are:

1. Tools: What you use to support, affect, and modify your life

2. Skillfulness: How well you engage tools, capacity, and connection

3. Capacity: Your ability to handle, or not happenings inside or outside of yourself

4. Connection: The reciprocal relationships that affect your growth, wellness, stability, awareness, understanding, needs, and overall sense of belonging

The Four Pillars, as you will see when you use them, all work with each other to lead to greater clarity and to fill out a complete picture for you. For example, you may be lacking a tool you need, like words to describe a feeling, but then you might not know how to find out what the word is, like your google searches don't help. So what do you do?

Maye you see, by referencing the Four Pillars, that skillfulness and capacity aren't the issue, just by process of elimination. So the last one, Connection, could be a resource. So you ask someone you trust if they can troubleshoot helping you find the word you need to describe the feeling you have. They may have a tool you don't know about or a skill you don't that they can share. This is the Connection pillar.

First and foremost, the way we engage the Four Pillars model is to utilize it. Meaning we need to remember it is there when we are triggered, stuck, down, anxious, hurt, confused, etc. So instead of using pathology models, religious models, new age models, or any other form of conditioning, we turn to the Four Pillars.

How we do this is by running down the list. So, Tools - is there a tool I need right now? Do I even know which tool I might need? Do I even know if there is a tool for this situation? Is there someone I can ask?

In a society that emphasizes "knowing", we often default to thinking we already know, somewhere in ourselves, what is needed for a situation. Or the person we are interacting with might assume we should know. By stepping back and asking "Do I know? Is this situation possibly a result of the possibility that I don't actually have a tool I need?" we open a world of empowered possibility for ourselves.

We do this, too, for skillfulness. So perhaps you have the tool. Say the tool, in the case of this book, is "Altar". And you have set up an altar but are finding yourself resistant or stuck. Then you ask "Is this a skilfulness issue?" Perhaps you find that, hey, I have no experience with an altar practice and have no idea what to expect and this is creating massive anxiety in me. So you accept the lack of skillfulness and start to address that. "Perhaps I could let myself be a beginner?" If this is the case, then do this. If the anxiety persists, assuming you have the tools, give yourself space to be a beginner, and still feel uncomfortable, move on to #3, Capacity.

Capacity is about our ability to hold or to handle the things we encounter. Think of it like how much space you have for what life is. Perhaps you have limited capacity for uncertainty. Perhaps you can be okay with being undeveloped in your skill, but your uncertainty is stressing you out because your capacity for uncertainty is low? Or maybe you are dealing with fear about what might happen if you actually encounter spirit-beings and you genuinely feel afraid of this?

You then play with this. Do you need practice growing your capacity? Is there someone - Connection - you could turn to? What do you need? Be curious and allow your creative self to engage here.

Play with these four areas to troubleshoot what you might need. If you can't figure it out, perhaps you share this with someone and ask for help? In other words, utilize Connection?

Many of us do not have healthy behaviors modeled for us. We are not given tools, taught how to practice, helped with growing our capacity, nor taught how to be relational in healthy ways. We are not taught to be curious or how to ask for help or how to think along the lines of relational support. So we need to shift from the pressure of knowing and "doing it right" to being able to learn whatever we might need to.

In order for us to get the most of the Four PIllars, we need to understand that some foundational things need to be cultivated, and certain attitudes need to be present:

- The necessity of experience
- Practice
- Curiosity
- Creativity
- Communication
- Research to understand basic needs, values, etc.
- Being gentle with ourselves
- To break the pathologizing habit
- Be Where You Really Are

As you go through this experience of Initiation, you might find the Four PIllars to be an invaluable aid in helping you navigate in a way that serves your journey, and you, without reinforcing, or getting ensnared, by the FOD.

Pick something from your own life and play with it through the Four Pillars model. Again, you are not trying to get it right, you are exploring to see where it leads, what insights or spaces might open up for you, even what stories you have been living in that you can begin to release or rewrite.

You will find that the Four Pillars all intersect and work together. Each pillar needs the others. People are often shocked to find out that they are lacking tools, like really basic tools, as adults. Like words. Words are a tool. Permission is a tool. Curiosity is a tool. We just assume we have tools or we assume the tools we have are sufficient and don't even wonder if the tools we use are the right ones for any given situation.

Be curious about your tools. Do you have the right tool? How do you know? Are there other tools? What happens if you are curious? What happens if you are willing to discover? Willingness is a tool. Perhaps you have a well-developed tool of "consciousness" that you use too often? Perhaps you did not know that innocence is sometimes a better tool to use, like when you are having an argument with someone you love?

We want to wonder about the things we take for granted, the things that are often invisible to us.

Fear is a very common reaction on the initiatory path. So

perhaps we wonder what Tool might be useful when fear arises. Or perhaps we wonder what being Skillful with fear might mean. Or perhaps we grow our Capacity for fear. Or perhaps we work with someone more experienced than us who might allay our fear (Connection).

Do you see how engaging the Four Pillars can allow us to exist in a way that is less bound by the dictates of the Field of Denial? How it might free us up to be more creative and effective in our own lives?

The initiatory path will be well served by utilizing the Four Pillars model, for it requires things of us that normal life, predictable life, conditioned life, simply does not.

So play with it. Explore it. Wonder about it. And see what emerges.

Thirty-three

THE DREAM SPACE

Dream space is where we can communicate most clearly with the beings of the Unseen. It is the space between our worlds where they can meet us, and we them.

Even people who say they "never dream", when they begin to connect with the Unseen, find that the dream space, where we go to meet with spirits, is alive and active for them and that they do, indeed, dream when they engage dreams as a form of spirit communication.

There are many techniques for utilizing the dream space as a spirit meeting place. Robin Artisson has done some excellent work on this, so you may want to explore his work. His book An Carow Gwynn contains a dream practice for obtaining answers from spirits and many of his other works talk about a technique he calls "shimmering". These are worth learning and utilizing.

So many people imagine that the way we encounter spirits will be obvious. And that, when it's not, it means they are somehow lacking or "doing it wrong".

Being able to hear, see, or otherwise sense spirits is not an "obvious" thing. This is why we work on embodiment and our felt sense, why we root and center, why we spend time in nature, why we make offerings, why we sit at our altars, why we venture into the woods and make pacts with strange beings, why we keep evidence journals, and why we dream.

The most common way to experience spirits for the majority of us is going to be through dreams. Please understand that this in no way diminishes the potency of the encounter. Dream space is a legitimate, bonafide, witchy, genuine encounter.

We must build our ability to communicate in dream space with the spirits. The ways we do this are varied. Each of us must find ways of what works best. What follows is a basic beginning.

Start by telling the spirits you desire to communicate with them. Tell them. Tell them the difficulties you might have, the obstacles you face, i.e. "I am unrooted and very conditioned" or "I never grew-up with nature as I was raised in a city and cannot hear trees or sense nature very well" or "I am really struggling with my health and finances and feel too burdened to sense you very well" or "our modern world says you aren't real and I never learned how to dream with you" or whatever it might be. Tell them and ask for help. Give offerings just to thank them for listening. Track that you have asked for help and, when you are aided, give more offerings in thanks. Do this at your altar or somewhere in nature where they might be closest to you.

As to dreaming....

You can, each night when you lay down to sleep, ask them

to communicate with you in your dreams. The most simple way to do this is to ask them a yes or no question. Then tell them what would constitute a yes. This means what will appear in your dream to indicate a yes. For example, you might say "If the answer is yes, then a rabbit or a stone or a sky will appear in my dream".

Then tell them the length of time this dream needs to happen within, like "over the next three nights". This way you do not set yourself up for failure by having no container and you give them time to come through. You could say just one night, but, especially if you are new to this, three nights is a good container. I always still say over the next three nights though my dreams most usually happen on the first night.

For some people it can be helpful to set an alarm that will wake them. Tell them this if you decide to do this. So 3:33 am or 6:36 am, just sometime when you will for sure be asleep and can be awakened by the alarm so that you can recall the dream.

Make sure to keep a way to record your dream near your bed and do not rely on memory. Much valuable insight has been lost to thinking we will recall a significant dream then going back to sleep. Do not rely on this. Keep a journal to record your dreams.

Learning to use the Dream Space this way can be a very rewarding experience. And a very useful way for us to build relationship with Them. As your dream space efforts "work", do put this in your evidence journal. Record what you ask, what you gave, what you promised, what you were shown.

Then you can begin to expand the ways you engage the Dream Space. You can make offerings to a particular being, say, your familiar. You can ask them to reveal themselves to you in a dream. You can ask to see them, for a name, and for any way they might work with you or guide you.

You can do this with land spirits, with beings known as deities, with ancestors, and more.

There is no limit, really, to how we might engage the dream space. You can ask for insight into an illness. You can ask for guidance on a particular issue. You can ask to be aided in the Dream Space.

Always remember to give offerings. Always remember to track what you ask for and to give back, both respect and gratitude and actual offerings, in return.

If you ask for something over a set period of time and you do not get a dream, the answer is "no". If you say "within 3 nights" and you get a dream the fourth night, the answer is "no".

Try to respect what you are told. Do not bug or bully or coerce or annoy. Be mature. None of us can know the reasons behind what we experience. Do not assume that you are not being supported if you do not get an answer you were hoping for.

The more you work with spirits, the more you deepen in

this path, the more likely your dreams begin to become quite potent. I think all witches, all people on this path, should keep a way to record their dreams and should do so regularly. They can be quite revealing.

Dreams as a form of spirit communication are a potent tool, one of the most potent we have. I advise you to research methods you can try and see which ones work for you.

Thirty-four

ALTARS

In Chapter 29 I give you guidance on setting up an ancestor altar practice, so I won't repeat that here. Instead, I want to talk about altars - what they are and why we might create, or utilize, them.

Altars can be found quite naturally all over the world in a great many number of different places. I'm sure most of you reading this have come upon altars in nature - places where you feel a presence and see something that looks "altar-y" - like a clearing at the base of a tree that has rocks in a strange pattern and acorns laying just-so and it just feels... *holy.*

You also probably have a lot of little altar spaces all over your house and in your car and you might make them wherever you go. We can't seem to help it, can we?

An altar is, by definition, a platform or table used as a center of worship. It is also a place sacrifices, or offerings, are made.

Many westerners have an issue with the word "worship". Especially those with overly religious upbringings where worship may have been shoved down their throats.

From etymonline.com we find the roots of the word Worship: Old English worðscip, wurðscip (Anglian), weorðscipe (West Saxon) "condition of being worthy, dignity, glory, distinction, honor, renown," from weorð "worthy" (see worth) + -scipe (see -ship). Sense of "reverence paid to a supernatural or divine being" is first recorded c. 1300. The original sense is preserved in the title worshipful "honorable" (c. 1300)

So our altars are a place of worship, where we honor beings we deem as having a condition of being worthy, having distinction or honor or renown. This serves ancestors, familiars, land spirits, and any other beings we honor.

On this path, getting past the conditioning of the FOD to be able to worship at our altars can take time. Many of us are filled with pride and we often conflate "worship" with groveling or being beneath or less-than.

If it helps to think of the spirit beings you encounter who are helpful, powerful, or that you care for like an ancestor or familiar as simply being worthy of honor, that is sufficient. If the word "worship" puts you off overly much, just substitute "honor".

Over time, as we worship at our altars, what begins to happen is that the altar itself becomes a kind of portal between realms - between the Seen and the Unseen. It also becomes a kind of beacon, where when we sit at our altars for long enough, and we do good works there, i.e. we give offerings, show respect, call out epithets, etc., that we are more easily found as the altar itself becomes a kind of *charged* space.

There is no one way to create an altar. Your altar may be beautiful to you or simply functional. It may be very plain or ornate. You may have altars for different purposes: one for ancestors, one for Hecate, one for necromantic workings, one for land spirits, etc.

I, personally, do not like overly fussy things. My altar is one space where I do all the things, assuming I am not doing a sacred working outdoors or that requires a larger space, like a circle of some kind.

My altar is simply a wooden shoe stand that has a top, a middle shelf, and room between the middle shelf and the floor. It is low to the ground. I use the shelves, including the floor as a shelf, to store my altar supplies and sacred items. My altar is on the top, which is covered with a beautiful cloth and a fur and various things like incense brazier, candles, and figures, then sacred items go on the middle shelf, while altar supplies, like a lancet for blood offerings, spare candle holders, incenses, oils, etc. all go on the floor "shelf".

I sit on some pillows so my aging body is as comfortable as possible. I use the wall my altar is up against for more altar-y things, like sacred images, a hawk wing, a deer skull, etc. I also have a small bookcase next to my altar where I keep my witchier books that are relevant to my altar work. So I have a variety of divination books, works of favored authors, some historical tomes I reference, etc.

While my altar is tucked into a little room, the room itself is made by some sheer curtains and shelving that separates it from the main room of the house. Meaning, it is right in plain sight as soon as you enter my living room. Anyone can see it. This does not bother me. Children often immediately go over to it and parents and other adults tend to be very cautious. As it is a place of worship, I am not overly precious about it being seen as I feel it is important that people experience such things. And I know many people do not ever see an established place of worship in a home, especially one that belongs to someone like me, as opposed to a Christian, for example.

You can locate, and regard, your altar however feels best to you. You can have as many or as few as you like. If you are going to combine altars, please do not put images of living beings on it when you do spirit work, especially ancestor work. What we put on our altars as spirit workers belongs, at least equally, to Them. We don't want anyone we love to be given over too soon.

With your altar, I will be assuming you will start with whatever makes sense to you and then you will educate yourself. Ideally, our personal education begins within our own lineages, with finding the indigenous traditions of our blood lines. For those of us of European descent, this means going back quite far, often over 1000 years, to find what we can about our own indigenous ancestors and their beliefs and practices.

Being that this likely means "before things were written down", we would also do well to look to folktales, folklore, herbal lore, etc. to glean insight into their minds and hearts.

I am big on blood lines, meaning I deeply value learning our own roots and connecting to them. We have the wisdom of the lands of our ancestors in our bodies. We would do well to learn what those lands are, and what they teach, and taught, the people we are related to. Each place has its own wisdom and ways and spirits. We honor them through our learning.

So here is another activity you can do at your altar that you can give as an offering or simply engage in: historical study, the reading of folktales, and researching herbal lore.

You will likely find that when you begin your relationship with the beings of the Unseen, that you can be very consistent then drop-off for weeks, even months, at a time with very little, if any, fall-out. But, over time, as the connection grows stronger, so, too, will the requirements of you to show up, to deepen your commitment and devotion, and to integrate, more and more, your spiritual life into your "regular" life.

You will begin to find a direct correlation between how well your life goes and how consistent and alive is your practice. Meaning, at first They tend to be lenient and patient, understanding this is new for you, but after some time, you will need to step it up. They will likely reveal this to you if you pay attention. Then you will need to step it up again, and again and again, until your spiritual practice is simply a way of life - that your awareness, and inclusion, of them is everywhere, always.

Your altar will arise however it does. And it will change over time. You may have a functional altar that is not very beautiful. You may need your altar to be beautiful. Or, perhaps, what makes it beautiful to you is its functionality.

Let your need of the space guide you. Set your altar up to first support its function. Is this an ancestor altar? A place to worship Aphrodite? A place for the Andedion? All of the above?

I often think of my ancestors who did not have access to the resources I do now. I think about candles. Maybe in the winter especially, a candle would serve multiple purposes - giving light in the evening, as a place for ancestral worship, to honor Brigid. I think of dishes and any other thing I might use as having been a part of their lives, not separate, but more practical. So I tend not to bring ideas of "purity" or exclusivity into my practice as regards these things. Meaning that I might use a small bowl for altar offerings one night, then use that bowl in my kitchen to mix a salad dressing the next day. I have few consecrated altar items, i.e. items that have been made sacred and exclusive to my spiritual practice. Some people choose to separate out the "mundane" from the "spiritual". Again, do what feels right to you now and change it as you feel to.

I certainly do have some ritual objects that have been created expressly for certain purposes that I keep on that middle shelf. I have divination tools that are consecrated to me, with my blood, that no one else will ever touch, at least, not while I am alive. But if I need a candle for something, and I have one on my altar that I've already used for something else, as long as that candle is not devoted to one being, I will use it for whatever the purpose at hand.

How you approach this is up to you. You will find your own way, and that way will change over time, given how alive this path is.

Do keep your altar clean. Unless you are working with a being who wants it otherwise, more chaotic or dirty for some reason, keep it clean.

The requirement for my altar to be clean is fairly high. I clean it as an offering to my ancestors and ancestral deities. They love it.

The room my altar is in also happens to be my Herb Lab - where I create potions and incenses and oils. The room itself can get quite messy, especially after a big creation burst. Sometimes the room will be messy for many days, until I recover from the burst and can clean it up. So my altar will be in that messy room for some time. This is my life and the reality of being me, at 54, with all that entails in my bones. I do the best I can and refuse to live under some stress about it, especially on my path. I get to be a person. I live BE WHERE YOU REALLY ARE. I recommend this.

As you deepen with your altar, with the things you do there, with it becoming a regular part of your life, you will begin to find that altars begin to *appear*, to materialize, right in front of you. You will be washing dishes and your sink turns into an altar, the act of washing the dishes sacred, the dishes themselves beings that aid your life in many ways that you see and appreciate and honor as you wash their bodies, the soap an anointing, the water a cleansing rite.

If you are not already living in a way where the Intelligence of LIfe, that is in and through all things, is alive within you, an altar practice will certainly awaken you to this. Relational aliveness will begin to emerge in your vision and your cells and you will simply walk differently through the world. This is a part of how we are remade, and our altar practice is central to this.

Thirty-five

EVIDENCE JOURNAL AS EMBODIMENT TOOL

I have mentioned the Evidence Journal in various places in this book. Here, I want to encapsulate its importance so that you will start one, regardless of how far on your path you are.

The Evidence Journal is a journal we keep of our lived experiences. It exists beyond, outside of, and in spite of the stories and beliefs and frameworks humans create and use.

What this means is that an Evidence Journal is a place where we *capture the communication and revelations of Life itself, as it reveals to us what it is.*

Do you understand how profound it is that we have moments in our lives where WHAT LIFE ACTUALLY IS shows itself to us? We have ways of seeing and understanding something that human beings have been chasing, and wrestling with, which is "understanding" itself.

We have overlaid a complexity of stories onto *what is* as we have also become increasingly unable to feel our own bodies as the interface organisms that we are.

In other words, *our bodies instantaneously feel Life's*

communication and we are able to perceive and understand this communication. And we have lost our conscious connection and honoring of the fact of this.

An evidence journal begins to heal this. It creates a kind of record of not only the phenomenology that the FOD says is impossible or irrational or delusional, but it also allows us to to begin to listen to our own intimate communication with Life because we begin to see, over and over and over, the aliveness and relational veracity of everything.

An evidence journal substantiates us in our bodies. It substantiates our belonging. It substantiates a larger reality. It substantiates the Dragon Mother beyond the invasion and erasure of the Field of Denial.

We keep an evidence journal as a physical record until we are reestablished within our own physicality.

It is not enough to feel your body. It is not enough to have "intuition" or to be "psychic". Being embodied in the way I am speaking to here means we feel the Intelligence of life as we are a part of that Intelligence. We do not feel it after, but as a part of. We do not get impressions, we are an arising of Intelligence and we are able to be aware and relational with this arising. This is what embodiment is. We do not think about it, we do not control it, we do not decide about it, it arises in us as we arise in each and every moment, one heaving interaction of everything inextricably complex.

We need a physical object that holds the facts of our lived experience because the mind and memory are nonsubstantive - they are not felt in the way a book or our bodies can be felt. We need something we can feel and see and interact with that will perform a surrogate embodiment until our own connection to the truth of our lived experience blossoms.

An Evidence Journal is the bridge. No belief, no hope, no framework will do what this will do for substantiating that the living intelligence, that *is* the Greater Intelligence, is in you and you are a belonging, crucial, undeniable part of the vast web of life.

In your evidence journal you will simply capture the facts of events that appear uncanny, miraculous, phenomenal, unexplainable, or just plain wyrd. You will mark the date and time if you know the time. Then you make your entry.

When I say report the facts, I mean you do not interpret as good or bad, you do not say things like "evil" or "wonderful", you simply write down what happened.

For example:

Tuesday December 15, 2009

I was at my altar, lit candles and gave offerings to ancestors. I was going to finish when I got the urge to sit longer. Suddenly I felt a surge of emotion and I began to pour my heart out. Tears came. I felt surprised at how powerful this was. I did not know I was holding so much in me. I found myself asking what I need to do since I feel so out of touch with my practice right now. I heard a word that sounded like "Freevthe". I finished my altar work and wrote down the word. I got on the internet and searched for the word. After much navigating, I found the word "freumh" which is a Scottish word that sounds exactly like the word that was said to me at my altar. Exactly. The word means "root". The wisdom of this lit up my body and I began to weep in gratitude. I went back to my altar and thanked Them and gave more offerings. I feel so deeply grateful and awed.

This is a made-up example of something that has actually happened to me quite a lot at my altar, where I ask a question and am answered in either Scottish, Welsh, or Old Norse. I speak none of these languages. But each time I ask a question and get a word(s) in another language and find that word, it is always exactly the most perfect answer to my question or need.

I do not try to "figure out" how this is possible. I do not make up any kind of a story. I simply exist in a state of awe and I make note of the fact of the experience. I do not try to explain it to myself. It happened, I note it. Yes, I feel thrilled. And I have had other experiences that are also beyond explanation that result in me feeling terrified. And I do not make up a story about this or try to explain it. I feel how I feel and I factually document the experience. Like having something breathe down the back of my neck with breath that is both palpable and hot and that smells wretched. I simply document this. I do not say it is bad or good, only that I felt scared.

Over time, these experiences begin to reveal things. We might learn hidden metaphysics. We might begin to understand something about spirits - familiars or plants or ancestors.

As we document these things, the signals of our bodies do not get interrupted, neutralized, or obliterated by our minds. We experience them, then we document the experience, then we have "proof" that we cannot head-trip our way out of. *This causes something profound to happen.*

And that profound thing is what you will experience as you dedicate yourself to keeping an evidence journal. It will change your life, and change you, in ways you cannot imagine. It will get you more connected more quickly than almost any single thing you can do.

If you couple the evidence journal with activities that increase your connection to the Unseen realm and to the beings of the Unseen, things will shift even more quickly.

Start one now. Document everything. Don't leave anything to memory because the FOD will obliterate it.

Thirty-six

TRUTH

I want to share some thoughts with you about truth as a way to help untangle from FOD conditioning. This perspective may help you shift in some profound ways, as well as create some space for your own becoming, and that of others.

Our society tends to hold invisible assumptions about truth: that it is a thing we must work to discover, and that truth is absolute.

I am speaking primarily of spiritual truths and truths we may come upon on our personal growth journey. I am not speaking of truth as synonymous with fact. Gravity is a fact. The existence, or not, of God is in the realm of truth.

What I've observed is that people tend to treat truth like it is an immovable object, or, rather, a place we arrive, like some grand temple with glowing, golden light streaming from it, or some chalice we drink from and become, ourselves, glowing and ever-smiling with bliss.

I would like to suggest this:

Truth is relevant to the pocket reality you occupy. Outside

of that pocket reality, there are other truths that are relevant to other places, to other pocket realities.

So what is true for you now, what is absolutely a lay-down-your-life-*knowing* of truth, can change.

As you navigate your own becoming on the initiatory path, you will arrive in places where the truths of that place will be so new or so different as to be uncomfortable, shocking, or even abhorrent.

You may find truths that do, indeed, bring you to tearful bliss. You may find truths that terrify you.

We must, each of us, do work to get to the point where we are no longer seeking truth but, instead, seeking *what is*.

Or, perhaps, we simply place the seeking of truth, and ideas about truth, lower on the priority list.

In an ever-unfolding moment, *what is*, is alive.

Truth tends to be, no matter how potent or truthy it is, not-alive, except in those moments where we experience the truth because it reveals itself in that moment where/when that truth actually exists.

The rest of the time that truth is belief we hold onto that very often serves the FOD.

When we seek relationship with the Dragon Mother, when we cultivate an embodied, ecosystemic responsiveness - aliveness, presence - truth is not a super relevant thing. At least, it's really not all that important.

If I see an animal (or plant or pond) suffering, what will likely come alive in me is care and concern for that animal (or plant or pond). Then that care will become in-formed in my entire being and I will act according to how that care guides me. I will not respond from an idea about "compassion" or "duty" or "rightness" or "being kind". I will respond from what comes alive in me. I will, first and foremost, *feel*.

The idea of living from truth, of being guided by truth, often results in not actually listening from within our bodies, but in playing out a role we are guessing at: "I believe in being a compassionate person so I am going to perform compassion on this situation..."

But what if the situation does not need your ideas about compassion? What if the situation needs something different and you, attached to your truth, do not listen?

All of us have caused harm with the "good intentions" that arise from our truth-performances.

I am not saying that living not-centered in truth, but instead in ever-unfolding responsiveness causes no harm. I am saying, however, that the harm caused is very likely to be more in line with what is needed at a level we cannot see or understand than us "performing truth" will ever be.

Many people feel anxious at the idea of not centering truth as the thing they seek and orient around. But as vessels for Her, as beings who belong within the greater ecosystem of life, there are situations we will encounter where we do what is required, not what we understand to be truth.

For example, I, as Sadee, may believe in being kind to people. But the Dragon Mother looking through me may need me to say something that is like slapping someone on the face. I may have an aversion to that slap, I may feel remorse for that slap, but I am likely going to say the thing She would have me say and deal with my feelings about it on my own. I have learned to hold this experience with a great deal of rooting and integrity, which often results in a person either not feeling assaulted or in feeling a sting but also feeling the truth in it. In other words, I have learned to be a vessel in a way that side-steps the FOD and touches the person directly.

I am not saying you should just immediately do this. Your ability to be a skillful vessel takes time, effort, and much more, to cultivate. You can see how easy it would be to be cruel or excuse bad behavior by taking this concept of being a vessel and letting the Less Self run with it.

Again, this path absolutely requires we cultivate personal accountability within the context of ecosystemic reality and utterly rooted in Her in an embodied, centered way.

Truth will meet you where you are, rather than you having to go out and find it, so you don't need to fuss about it.

When truth is centered as a priority, the Field of Denial floods in. It opens the gates to all the off little dynamics that the human-created realm thrives on: power-trips, exclusivity, hierarchy, secrets, access, guru-ship and cults.

If I claim truth, truth that feels truthy to you, truth you don't seem to have as much access to as I do, and I gate-keep that truth, I make it so you must come to me to get this truth and that I will always have more of that truth than you, no one is learning anything. Everyone is just playing a FOD game.

The idea of truth-as-priority feeds into arrogance. It makes people feel potent and better-than. And when it is an invisible assumption - when the primacy of truth is treated as preeminent - a lot of shenanigans arise. Having truth makes folks feel important. Having truth makes folks feel special. Having truth gets people money. Having truth fosters hierarchies.

The reality is that any genuine truth we encounter arises from relational responsiveness. It is not a static belief that we overlay onto life. Truth, genuine truth, is the fabric of reality itself. It is nothing more than this. It is not aspects of that fabric of reality removed from relational context and gussied up into a fancy story that serves our smallness, our fears, our power hunger, our denigration of nature, our inability to handle what life is. We need tools and skills and support to deal with what life is. But to turn that into a hunt for truth, where it is implied that truth is a savior of some kind, is harmful and wrong. And that is exactly what the Field of Denial does with it.

The initiatory path is concerned with bringing you ever-more-deeply into relationship with the Dragon Mother. This seems to result in making you a much better person.

But not "better" according to the Field of Denial, better according to the many other beings you exist with. Indeed, the Field of Denial will very much want to demonize or denigrate you for not participating in its truth-centering. People who are very much aligned with the FOD will likely be incapable of seeing that truth is not the center around which one should pivot and will desire to get into reality battles with you, "reality battles" being where we pit our truths against each other and see which one triumphs.

I want to be clear that I am speaking about truth that is based in belief, thought, and arrogance. I am not saying "there is no truth". There is a truth that is in accordance with reality. And by this I mean Primal Reality - the reality that exists in spite of the human-created, that all of life participates in according to its rhythms and Intelligence. There is no "pure" state we, in our lifetimes, will achieve with this. Modern life is what it is. But we *can* take what we learn and see and experience every single day when our eyes and bellies and cells are open and listening to the life around us, beneath the noise of the FOD, and, if you are quite keen, within it as well, and live from the truths that Intelligence reveals and urges in us.

The paradox is: there is absolutely truth, it is crucial, and that truth is most relevant and alive in each and every moment as-it-is, according to what the ecosystem of being requires. Truth is not a static thing we carry in us and overlay onto the life around us. We know the truth not as knowledge we gain, but truth as ones who are alive with it. It is our work to learn to feel with discernment and to get out of the way of this holy Life as it moves us, with it, as one mighty river.

Thirty-seven

WHEN AM I A WITCH

I know I spoke about being a witch in the chapter about the Black Path. I am going to write more, and even repeat some things, here because of how much energy there is around this word these days.

It's very popular these days to call oneself a witch. From the variety of ways I see it used, it seems a witch is anything someone claims it to be. While I'm not going to gatekeep the word, I am going to tell you what I believe a witch to be and why, to me, the term is sacred and should be treated as such. Take from it what you will.

A witch is someone who has gained a degree of kinship with Them of the Unseen. Witches have earned protection and some form of help or favor from the Good Folk.

This isn't about crystals or hexing or power or spells. This is about one's relationship with the land, the ecosystem, and being in right-relationship with at least *some* spirits - that those spirits watch out for you and keep you safe in places that other people either wouldn't dare go or would need to take some kind of (occult) measures to stay safe.

To me, a witch is one who works with spirit beings in a reciprocal, right-relationship kind of way. What I would call a witch is one who is respectful and careful and aware of the Unseen realm and seeks to learn from the beings of the Unseen how to be with them and how to be in this world.

This is because when we enter into a right-relationship, when we learn from the beings of the Unseen, something begins to happen, something *strange*.

We begin to become something else, we become transformed, made into *more than* just human - we become *witched*. You can call yourself anything you want. But becoming witched is to be made different - to be made more like *Them*.

While we may pursue being a witch, may seek this out, to be truly witched is not, ultimately, our decision. We are made this way through our relationship(s) with Them of the Unseen.

Doing spells, or not, using crystals, or not, having an altar, or not, none of these mean anything outside of the greater ecosystem of beings. What matters is how we treat the beings of the Unseen, how they regard us, and the favor we are shown by Them because we are in relationship with Them.

This doesn't mean all of the Unseen. I mean personal, intimate relationship like you would have with a close friend or lover. They know you and you know them because they teach, reveal, guide, and protect you. You meet them in dreams, speak with them, perhaps, for some, even have some kind of physical or sexual relationship.

I have encountered thousands of people who call themselves witch. Very few of them are actually *witched* - have actually been made strange through their relationship with the Good Neighbors - Them of the Unseen - and been transformed into something more-than-human.

This is my view, my belief, and what I know to be true. Witch has become just a word, a hot, trendy word that makes people feel good to say. I know there are sincere souls who simply do not have knowledge that would guide them to the Unseen, to right-relationship, but have true hearts. I respect that. And I have guided many of these folks down the path of becoming witched should they choose to walk it. I also know that people become witched without knowing this is happening, but just through their relentless devotion to this path. I believe becoming witched is foundational to this Initiatory Path - we are able to serve Her because we become more like Her.

If you truly belong to Her, you will, at some point, become witched. Her path makes you *strange*, if you aren't already.

Thirty-eight

MOVING FORWARD

Throughout this book, you have undoubtedly asked, at various points, "How?". And I have repeatedly answered "Go to Them and learn". This is the best, wisest answer, frustrating though it may be. It does not mean it is the only one.

I have given various techniques to employ - from Be Where You Really Are to an Evidence Journal and much in between. I know that many of the suggestions I have given may lack a certain "wow" factor or may seem overly basic, especially if you have been on this path for some time, or you are imagining it needs to be a certain way. Do not be fooled by the simplicity.

The simplest things, the foundational things, are the ones that are the most difficult to master and lead to the greatest change. You can take my word for it or you can learn this on your own.

The simple practices in this book will absolutely lead to incredible, unexplainable, magical experiences. They will also grow your ability to walk this path.

While you are incorporating, in whatever way works for you, the information in this book, I want to give you a bit more here in this last chapter.

You will be greatly aided on your path by knowing the following:
1) Exposure to someone who truly belongs to Her will have an accelerating effect on you
1) Research and study are invaluable
2) Trial and error are essential

Let me say a bit more about each of these.

Being in relationship with someone who truly belongs to Her will have an accelerating effect on you. There are a couple of reasons for this:

One is that the field around someone who has been made truly strange, who truly *belongs to Her*, contains a markedly different reality than the FOD. Strange things are made possible, strange experiences are amplified, contact with the Unseen is made more manifest, when we are around someone who is witched.

Another reason for this is that the Dragon Mother will speak to you through this person. The things said to you will often come from Her, according to your need and your Wyrd, through the body of Her vessel. These words and experiences will have an altering effect on your own field. They will cause events to occur, things to shift, your reality to be altered just by proximity to this person. This can be physically near or far. It need not be in-person.

You will get a true taste of the veracity of Primal Intelligence. Your mind will be blown. Things will become possible for you that were not possible before this encounter. This person's presence will activate, and amplify, your own initiatory journey.

Treat this person with the honor and respect they deserve and resist the urge to overly lay claim to what awakens in your life after you encounter one such as this. Too many people, bound as they are to the Less Self and the Field of Denial, are unable to acknowledge the gift they are given and claim, instead, themselves to be the sole activators and source of their new- found abilities and insights. This serves no one as it reinforces the notion of non-relational reality and self-serving untruths that then also block others from being able to access the Dragon Mother because it turns people's focus to the individual who appears to have power and to overly focus on that one and then themselves for their own healing and becoming. This perpetuates the FOD and violates the truth of ecosystemic complexity, nuance, and power.

Hopefully the person you work with who belongs to Her is mature and capable of honoring you as you walk your path and does not try to overly claim responsibility for what you accomplish. Hopefully there is right-relationship between you and each of you bows to Her as the main source of both of your truths and power rather than having resentment or power-struggle with one another. Acknowledgement is a human need. May this be truly balanced and healthy between you and your teacher/mentor/guide.

Research and study are invaluable. There is an incredible amount of really good information if you go and look for it.

There are many humans who are truly strange who have made available their wisdom and research for you to utilize and benefit from.

History is definitely a good path. Learning the latest understanding through the fields of archeology and linguists and folklorists and more will all benefit you.

Explore diverse views so you can feel which ones light up in your body and follow those. Your signal will become honed and you will see themes emerging.

Do remember what it looks like when we get pulled - like a messy scribble of appearing "all over the map". Try not to get overly attached to what you are pulled to, but view these things as breadcrumbs that lead you with wisdom you likely cannot see or understand.

Look into the mythology of place of your ancestors and their ancestors. Endeavor to understand how migration and colonization and intermingling can influence, erase, and transform cultures and ways of people so you do not get overly attached to notions of historical purity or idealism.

Realize that we cannot know the minds of our ancestors or of the indigenous people we come from. But we can immerse ourselves in whatever remains of their world and, in this way, give context to the mighty web of life and spirit beings that we may be informed and transformed by in truly profound ways that serve to separate us from the clutches of the FOD and possibly integrate us more reply into *what is.*

Trial and error are essential. As has been said many times in this book, let us release ideas of "right" and "knowing" so that we might become curious and truly learn. This means we allow ourselves to experiment.

So try the spell, do the ritual, follow your intuition and see what happens. Some of us dive into the deep end and others dip in toes. Be where you really are. But do experiment.

This is how we not only find what we are truly drawn to, but how we create a foundation that allows us to understand the elements of sorcerous workings, magical workings, spirit workings, healing workings, oracular workings, enough to be able to create our own workings.

Each step we take toward strange experiences has the potential to transform us. The initiatory path is a path of transformation. What we are confronted with during trial and error can radically shift or open or change us in ways we cannot imagine.

I often tell people that we are blessed to not know what we are getting into when our fire and enthusiasm and naivete win out and we plunge into this path. It is often when it is too late that we realize what we have done and cannot go back. This, too, is part of this path. We are pulled into what we need, which is not always what we might want. There is wisdom in this as well as caution.

This journey is a constant attentiveness to how we are pulled, cultivating discernment, and learning what this path even is. We must constantly come up for air and look around and take stock so that the parts of us that might need the pace to slow can be tended to.

Many of us come to this path wounded or not knowing how to properly care for ourselves with love and softness, so we throw ourselves into places that not all aspects of us might be okay with.

Any healthy relationship is about both parties being cared for and tended to. We do not martyr ourselves to Her. We are transformed, yes, to give and be more and more and more *for Her*, but at no point is sacrifice a demand in the way so many are conditioned to believe.

Because this path is relational, we can communicate our needs and our modern situation and our ignorance. Like any healthy relationship, it depends on communication. Do not treat the beings of the Unseen like omnipotent mind readers. Just as that doesn't work with anyone you've ever met in the flesh, it doesn't tend to work with beings who do not have flesh.

We need to be mature. We need to be relational. We need to communicate. We need to participate. We need to become different from what we are.

All of these things take practice based on personal accountability.

So often we think overly much about doing the thing and do not invest enough exploration into whether or not we are even capable of doing the thing. This is not kind of us to do to ourselves. And it is ignorant.

This path requires maturity and skillfulness and more. It is an amazing truth that walking this path grows us into people who can walk the path. She has a way of being that kind of genius. The more we walk this path, the more we are grown into people who can walk it, and the more we must walk it for our lives to work for us. It is truly brilliant and beautiful.

Initiation is complex, dizzying, life-threatening, and magnificent. It is my hope that the words and spirit in these pages aids you on your journey.

I invite you to join me on my website where I will be hosting a safe community for Witches, Healers, and other Strange Creatures to offer a sacred space for connection, support, and education to further aid you as you engage this most incredible phenomenon called Life.

Thank you for reading. I truly wish you the best in the trials and exaltations that are the Savage Awakening journey.

Please visit the Resource section for more.

RESOURCES

Below you will find a smattering of resources to explore. This list is not comprehensive, rather, it expresses a small variety of voices and perspectives I have found interesting.

TheDragonMother.com - For Witches, Healers, and Other Strange Creatures. This is my own website. Please check frequently for offers, courses, and membership information.

Robin Artisson - Anything this strange creature creates
Website: RobinArtisson.com
Books:
An Carow Gwynn

The Witching Way of the Hollow Hill

The Clovenstone Workings

The House of the Giantess

The Secret History

Letters from the Devil's Forest: An Anthology of Writings on Traditional Witchcraft, Spiritual Ecology and Provenance Traditionalism

Lee Morgan: LeeMorganBooks.com
Book:
A Deed Without a Name: Unearthing the Legacy of Traditional Witchcraft

Emma Wilby:
Books:
Cunning Folk and Familiar Spirits: Shamanistic Visionary Traditions in Early Modern British Witchcraft and Magic

Visions of Isobel Gowdie: Magic, Witchcraft and Dark Shamanism in Seventeenth-Century Scotland

Roger J. Horne
Book:
Folk Witchcraft: A Guide to Lore, Land, & the Familiar Spirit

Derrick Jensen
Book:
The Myth of Human Supremacy

Steve Silberman
Book:
NeuroTribes: The Legacy of Autism and the Future of Neurodiversity

David Abram
Book:
The Spell of the Sensuous: Perception and Language in the More-Than-Human World

Hans Dieter Betz
Book:
The Greek Magical Papyri in Translation

Jack Grayle
Book:
The Hekataeon

Red K. Elders
Art:
Redkelders.bigcartel.com

Marian Woodman and Elinor Dickson
Book:
Dancing in the Flames: The Dark Goddess in the
Transformation of Consciousness

Claude Lecouteux
Books:
Demons and Spirits of the Land: Ancestral Lore and
Practices

Claudia Müller-Ebeling, Christian Rätsch, Wolf-Dieter Storl
Book:
Witchcraft Medicine: Healing Arts, Shamanic Practices,
and Forbidden Plants

Raven Kaldera and Galina Krasskova
Book:
Neolithic Shamanism: Spirit Work in the Norse Tradition

Barbara Tedlock
Book:
The Woman in the Shaman's Body: Reclaiming the

Feminine in Religion and Medicine

ACKNOWLEDGEMENTS

Sydnor Hain-Fawzi - your editing, insights, comments, and sharing of the impact the book had on you as you read it was like wind beneath my wings. Thank you for the immense amount of time and energy and love you put into this. https://www.AwakePowerfulFree.com/

Rhiannon Hasenauer - I think you were the very first person with which I ever shared any of my earliest pages of this book! Your excitement, light, and affirming "Fuck Yes!" added light to my fire and anchored me in the face of endlessly daunting blank pages. That you needed this book helped me to write it. Thank you for your sweetness and endless support. https://MotherlineMagic.com

Maya Luna - It has been so fun to share how She is working with and through you. Your own initiatory journey has been exceptional to witness and participate in - I deeply respect your strength, determination, courage, brilliance, and magic. It has been so fulfilling, beyond words, to be able to witness your transformation and blossoming and to talk about the strangest, deepest aspects of what this path is. I appreciate your feedback and encouragement and fire about this book, the oracle deck, and my work, and that you reached out, what feels like years ago, though it has been far less. You are truly of the Red Path, truly Hers, and I am so excited for anyone reading this book to seek out your work, your poetry, your book, and your embodiment offerings: https://DeepFeminineMysterySchool.com

Kaelin Kerr - the conversations with you are always so fun and alive! I so appreciate your feedback and enthusiasm about the book! It gave me energy when I needed to write and I thought of you so often in these many chapters. I hope this completed book brings you clarity, companionship, and guidance on your path. Find her on Etsy: TheArtsyMythic

I want to thank my clients over these many decades. You all have allowed me to grow and develop and practice being Her vessel. To those of you that trusted me with the vulnerable truths of your initiatory experiences when others labeled you unwell, thank you. There is nothing more beautiful to me than seeing people awaken to their home in Her, and to bring to others the fruits of their devotion, trials, and courage. I have the deepest love and respect for you all.

Thanks, also, to the many good folks on Facebook who have offered opinions, encouragement, enthusiasm, feedback, and have generally been a great support and sounding board for me. I so appreciate that you have spent your precious time and energy on my page.

To my mom, April, I would not be who I am without you. You have always fiercely supported, encouraged, and defended me being the little wyrdo that I am. Thank you for letting me practice foot reflexology on you when I was 8. Thank you for always being willing to taste my potions. Thank you for letting me practice energy work on you. Thank you for calling me from across the country to get rid of your headaches even though you never understood how it worked, only that it did and you always just accepted I'm like this. Thank you for meeting me in the fire I have brought to your life. Thank you for loving me as I am. I know it has taken everything you have to be my mom and you have done it with incomprehensible grace, power, and ferocious love. I could never have become half of what I am if it weren't for you. I love you more than words will ever be able to say.

No acknowledgement would be complete without thanking my sweet love, Alexander. Your endless support, making me tea, talking with me about concepts in the book, giving me feedback, cleaning the house so I could write, and the million other ways you have loved, supported, and helped me - I could not have written this book without your love and belief. You have made me a better Hag and human. Walking this path together has been one of the most special experiences of my life. I love you, always, and no matter what.

ABOUT THE AUTHOR

Sadee Whip lives in the forested outskirts of a small town in western Washington. She spends her days drinking tea, writing, teaching, reading, and spending far too much time at her altar. She can be found getting up to various shenanigans in her herb lab, her garden, her kitchen, and the woods she frequents.

Sadee has spent her entire life in devotion to the path she walks and is crammed chock-full of a staggering breadth of knowledge and experience that she shares in various ways. Please visit her at: TheDragonMother.com

Printed in Great Britain
by Amazon

59273850R00175